Pentecostalism and Catholic Ecumenism In Developing Nations

Pentecostalism and Catholic Ecumenism In Developing Nations

West Africa as a Case Study for a Global Phenomenon

JOHN SEGUN ODEYEMI

Foreword by Paschal John Chibuzo Nwaezeapu

WIPF & STOCK · Eugene, Oregon

PENTECOSTALISM AND CATHOLIC ECUMENISM IN DEVELOPING NATIONS
West Africa as a Case Study for a Global Phenomenon

Copyright © 2019 John Segun Odeyemi. All rights reserved. Except for brief quotations in critical publications or reviews, no part of this book may be reproduced in any manner without prior written permission from the publisher. Write: Permissions, Wipf and Stock Publishers, 199 W. 8th Ave., Suite 3, Eugene, OR 97401.

Wipf & Stock
An Imprint of Wipf and Stock Publishers
199 W. 8th Ave., Suite 3
Eugene, OR 97401

www.wipfandstock.com

PAPERBACK ISBN: 978-1-5326-7645-1
HARDCOVER ISBN: 978-1-5326-7646-8
EBOOK ISBN: 978-1-5326-7647-5

Manufactured in the U.S.A. APRIL 23, 2019

In Memoriam

Very Rev. Fr. Francis Olabanji Adeponle
Born July 12, 1957
Ordained September 1, 1984
Died August 29, 2013

&

Very Rev. Fr. Cosmas 'Femi Aina
Born August 2, 1963
Ordained August 13, 1994
Died April 16, 2012

May you now enjoy the reward of the just.

The publication of this book is made possible
through the generosity of Missio Aachen

Contents

Foreword by Paschal John Chibuzo Nwaezeapu | ix
Acknowledgements | xiii
Introduction | xvii

1. Report on Fieldwork, Research Findings, and Data Analysis | 1
2. Ecumenism | 17
3. Pentecostalism | 36
4. Catholic Ecumenism | 64
5. Pentecostalism and Ecumenism in West Africa | 83
6. Review and Recommendations | 97

Appendix A: Figures | 109
Appendix B: Sample Questionnaires I & II | 121
Bibliography | 129
Index | 133

Foreword

THAT PENTECOSTALISM IN ITS various forms is spreading out to the different parts of the world, especially Africa, Asia, and South America is no longer news. But, what do you think? Is Pentecostalism a cog in the wheels of ecumenical works or a part of the "new Pentecost"? This is central to the work you are about to read. In his book, *Pentecostalism and Catholic Ecumenism in Developing Nations: West Africa as a Case Study for a Global Phenomenon*, John Segun Odeyemi tries to examine the state of ecumenism today in light of the widespread proliferation of Pentecostalism, using the experience of West Africa as a case study.

Going through the work, two questions which are central to his thesis continue to ring a bell in my head. Is Pentecostalism a cog in the wheel of ecumenical works in West Africa or in other places? Why has Pentecostalism emerged as a global force to reckon with, necessitating the first question?

In West Africa, especially Nigeria and Ghana, Pentecostalism is very popular as the author acknowledges and we cannot deny the fact that a good number of the founders of the different Pentecostal churches are motivated by selfish or worldly considerations, such as money and fame. Even though the continuous multiplication of these churches will present some challenges, Pentecostalism in itself may not necessarily be a cog in the wheel of ecumenical works in the region, depending on the approach and openness of all the parties involved. In spite of some serious disagreements that may arise from time to time, if all the parties involved adopt an attitude of humility, respect for the other, complete openness to the truth, and what the Holy Spirit is saying to the churches, ecumenism will not only succeed, but all the churches involved will be better enriched. So, the real challenge is whether all the participants are willing to succumb to the truth and what the Spirit is saying, or to worldliness and what the self is saying.

Foreword

Now, let me focus on the second issue. About thirty years ago, Pentecostalism was not popular in Nigeria, and I believe that the same is true of other West African countries. The question I think the leaders of the traditional established churches and every committed Catholic should be asking is, "Why has Pentecostalism grown in such a short period to become so popular among the people?"

There are two ways to look at this phenomenon. The first is what I consider an easy way out, while the second is a more realistic approach to the emergence and popularity of Pentecostalism. The easy way involves castigating the founders of the different Pentecostal churches as capitalizing on the ignorance and the naivety of the poor people in the developing countries to manipulate them in order to enrich themselves. No doubt, we cannot completely deny that, going by our experience of Pentecostalism in West Africa. But then, the problem with this easy approach is that it is narrow and non-exhaustive of the evidence on ground. For example, in addition to the poor people in question, many of the established Pentecostal churches boast of many well-educated, "enlightened," wealthy, and fulfilled members, which explain why they have become affluent. In reality, Pentecostalism comes with its own baggage as the author acknowledges, and besides, the further splintering of the Christian church is never desirable. But to reduce the phenomenon of Pentecostalism merely to a form of enslavement of the poor and oppressed people, as some people tend to claim, will be a hasty generalization and an easy way out in my candid opinion.

A more realistic approach to the rapid growth and popularity of Pentecostalism in West Africa and other parts of the globe will be a critical self-examination on the part of the Catholic Church and the other traditional churches, with regard to our mission of evangelization. For some years, I have been investigating the reasons why many Catholics and others in Nigeria are drifting to the Pentecostal churches and the revelation is quite instructive.

Contrary to what some people think, most of the more enlightened Catholics are not drifting to Pentecostalism because of the prosperity gospel or miracles, but for other serious reasons. These include: their ability to lead them from sheer religiosity to a personal relationship or communion with God, spiritual fulfillment in worship, music, teaching them to read the Bible daily, addressing their concrete day-to-day experiences within society, and empowering them (through the building up of their personal faith in God) to survive in a typical African society where people contend daily, not just with economic hardship, but also with (either perceived or real) spiritual attacks from witches and wizards, cultists, fetish practices by enemies, and so on. Furthermore, some of them claim that their new churches have opened their eyes to the spiritual gifts or *charisms* (such as healing, teaching, words of knowledge, prophecy, and so on) which have remained latent in them because they were never told about them or activated in their former churches. Discovering and using these gifts has brought enormous fulfillment to many of them, thereby enabling them to fulfill their role in the church's mission. Other important reasons for the drift of Catholics to Pentecostalism is ignorance of the Catholic faith by most Catholics arising from poor catechesis, absence of disciple-making programs, and the lack of emphasis on the charismatic dimension of the church, which often results in the disempowerment of the lay faithful who make up over 99 percent of the population of the church.

My point here is that our failure in the area of evangelization which is our mission as a church is the most significant reason for the rise and popularity of Pentecostalism. The four stages of our mission of evangelization are witness (pre-evangelization), *kerygma* (initial proclamation) with its goal as conversion, catechesis or disciple-making with its goal as the transformation of individuals to become Christ-like, and mission or apostleship. If we are achieving the goals of this evangelization process in the church, then we should be raising a generation of Catholics who are real soldiers or missionary disciples who know God experientially (from an intimate personal relationship with him); who proclaim him from a personal conviction; who witness to Jesus by striving to replicate his lifestyle and make other disciples for him. But unfortunately, we have been raising more of "mechanical" Catholic Christians and sacramentalizing and confirming people who may never have been properly evangelized and converted in their minds and hearts as Pope Saint John Paul II once observed. Was that not why he launched the Universal Church into a new evangelization in 1990? But what has changed in most places since then as far as Mission *ad gentes*, new evangelization, and pastoral care are concerned? As it is often said, "nature abhors a vacuum." In spite of its own baggage, Pentecostalism, in its positive form, is and will continue to fill the vacuum in our people if we do nothing significant to fill it ourselves.

This book by John Segun Odeyemi, beyond addressing some of the issues that arise in the field of ecumenical works in the light of Pentecostalism, offers us a new opportunity to rethink our poor attitude to the church's

Foreword

mission, viewed from both its strict sense and the big picture of Christianizing the culture in society. The book is a must read and I heartily recommend it to all, especially all church leaders, the entire clergy, religious, lay leaders in the church, and the laity as a whole. I congratulate John for the enormous contributions embodied in this well-researched piece of work.

Msgr. Paschal John Chibuzo Nwaezeapu
Divine Mercy Catholic Church, Lekki,
Lagos, Nigeria
October 4, 2018
Feast of St. Francis of Assisi

Acknowledgements

No matter how small in scope a project such as this might be, oftentimes you encounter many people along the way who lend a helping hand to get the researcher through many hoops. In doing the fieldwork for this research, I was very fortunate to meet such people, some I have had the pleasure of knowing before now and others were new acquaintances. To everyone who gave me a helping hand through this process, mentioned here or not, I am indeed grateful and God's blessings upon you all.

GHANA

Before ever going to Ghana, I made contact with Bishop John Bonaventure Kwofie, CSSp, who was newly appointed as bishop of the diocese of Sekondi/Takoradi. And early this year, 2019, was appointed Archbishop of Accra, Ghana. He was extremely gracious, despite a busy schedule, which included an immediate trip to Rome and the United States to set up accommodation and contacts for me in Accra. Fr. Michael Mensah of St. Paul's Major Seminary, Sowutuom-Accra was gracious with his time and contacts within the Pentecostal family in Accra. I am greatly indebted to Bro. Constant Tagyang, CSSp: Provincial Bursar, Spiritan Provincialate, Adenta-Accra. He went out of his way to provide me with room and board, show me around Accra, and drove me to series of appointments. Bro. Tagyang showed me a humble, simple, and down-to-earth servant of Christ. Without him, the work in Accra would have been impossible.

Acknowledgements

IVORY COAST

All arrangements were made for me in Cote d'Ivoire by l'Abbe Clement Abiodun, an older brother priest. I was given accommodation at parish of Notre Dame de l'Esperance. I am indeed grateful to the parish priest, Pere Louis Nanchot, his curates, Peres Judicael and Anderson, and the parish staff who were overgenerous with their hospitality for the two weeks I was resident in their parish. Three young men were assigned to drive me around, and even drove me over three-hundred miles to see the Cathedral at Yamassuokro: Petit Baoule, Kouakou Olivie, and Amidou Kone. I thank all the good people of Notre Dame de Lourdes parish, Abatta village. All your kindness and efforts are truly appreciated.

SIERRA LEONE

My first thanks and appreciation must go to the SMA Fathers at KWAMA. Through the connection of longtime friend and brother priest, Fr. Patrikson Francis, I met Frs. David and Vallery Aguh, both his SMA associates and collaborators. They took it upon themselves to drive me several times from Kwama to Freetown and to make the necessary contacts for my work. I can gladly say that Sierra Leone was the most successful in terms of conducting interviews and the application of questionnaires. I must also thank, most sincerely, his grace, Archbishop Charles Tamba of Freetown. He welcomed me at the cathedral and was exceptionally cordial every time I ran into him at some other functions—an ebullient and untiring pastor, ready to dance, laugh, and sing with his people. My time in Sierra Leone remains essential to the writing of this book. I am grateful to you all.

LAGOS

Very Rev. Msgr. Philip Hoteyin and Very Rev. Fr. Anthony T. Fadairo at St. Agnes, Maryland, Lagos were my landlords at any time I was in Lagos or passing through. I will remain ever grateful for the ways in which they made their homes available to me. I also remain grateful to Mr. Tunde Aina, who on several occasions had to show me around Lagos and bring me to Pentecostal churches where I sought audience with pastors and founding fathers. I thank him for his time, resources, and patience. I appreciate Mr.

Acknowledgements

Aina's patience the most when having to deal with the traffic in Lagos, and what seemed at the time, an effort that was not going anywhere.

IBADAN

Very Rev. Fr. Ezekiel Ade Owoeye, parish priest of Our Lady Seat of Wisdom University Catholic Parish, University of Ibadan, Nigeria. He was essential to the realization of this book project. He gave suggestions, both practical and logistical, as to the best ways to achieve the fieldwork that had literally failed in Lagos. He also provided bed and board and a vehicle to use all through the times I was working in Ibadan. In the same vein, I must thank Mr. Dominic Awofusi who was very generous with his time. He drove me tirelessly to many appointments, some of which ended up as a total waste of time. Your patience and understanding are deeply appreciated.

I am grateful to his eminence, John Cardinal Onaiyekan, metropolitan archbishop of Abuja. He squeezed out time from an overcrowded schedule to sit down with me at the very beginning of this project and, from his wealth of experience in interreligious dialogue at home and all over the world, he showed me some of the cultural, historical, and political problems hindering ecumenical work at home (Nigeria), on the continent and internationally. His insights helped in shaping most of this work. I must also thank my friends at Missio Aachen who gave the much-needed funds to undertake the traveling needed for the fieldwork for this book. Missio's work continues to inspire the Catholic Church in developing nations of the world.

I thank Bess Biamonte and Deacon Anton Mobley, friends who were my first level editorial sounding board. Your comments and attention to details, your sacrifice of time, and talent are a great part of completing this project. Also, to my friend Michele Fagan who constantly reminded me to get back to my desk and write: thank you. Special thanks to Irene Lahr, Frs. Anselm Jimoh, PhD, Francis Kunle Adedara, PhD, and Dr. Rufus Burnett Jnr, Dr. Joyce Konigsburg, Toritseju Omaghomi (Doctoral Candidate, University of Cincinnatti), who analyzed the raw data and put them into graphs. Thanks to everyone for all the different ways in which your friendship brings me so much joy.

JOHN SEGUN ODEYEMI, PHD
Church of the Epiphany,
Uptown Pittsburgh

Introduction

MODERN ECUMENISM AND PENTECOSTALISM are two different phenomena, which have occurred in the Christian world in the last hundred years. In principle, ideas that resonate with modern ecumenism and Pentecostalism abound from the early Christian communities of the Acts of the Apostles and the different early Christian eras. Contemporary ecumenism and Pentecostalism from their very origins have shown themselves to be complex, especially when they are related to traditional orthodoxy of established Christian churches, Catholics East and West, Catholic-Protestant and Orthodox-confessional faiths, and now the charismatic/Pentecostal churches.

Modern ecumenical movement is inspired by a vision of a possible unity in mission, evangelism, and common witness among the various denominations of the Christian churches today. The ecumenical unions work for a possible unity of Christian churches in one faith, one eucharistic fellowship of worship, and a common Christian life. It is not at any time to be misunderstood as a synonym for a structural merger, but a unity in diversity, a unity in pluriformity. These efforts have taken on a universal form within the last century, with world ecumenical meetings and a centralized body in Geneva, Switzerland. This led to the birth of the World Council of Churches (WCC) in 1948.

The Pentecostal phenomenon has enjoyed great followership in developing nations, especially, it would seem, at the expense of the traditional established Christian churches. The Pentecostal focal points include some of the following themes: a new approach to community, miraculous healings, expulsion of demons, speaking in tongues, the gift of prophecy, spontaneous prayers, baptism and experience of the Holy Spirit, financial breakthrough, and material wealth. Even though it was criticized initially by the established churches as theologically unsystematic, lacking in doctrine and

Introduction

dogma, its appeal and rate of growth remains ever on the upward curve. This growth is now recognized and acknowledged among the World Council of Churches as perhaps the "new Pentecost" of our age. The presence and appeal of Pentecostalism is noticed more in developing or underdeveloped countries of Africa, Asia, and South America, which has made it a force to be reckoned with.

Pentecostalism may be popular, but it has a considerable baggage of problems to deal with. For now, a brief reflection suffices: Pentecostalism is a proliferation and further splintering of the Christian church that was born out of the sixteenth century Reformation. As young as it is within Christianity and the history of the Southern Hemisphere, Pentecostalism itself continues to suffer multiplications and splintering or breakaway factions. In all of the West African countries I visited, the most notorious are Ghana and Nigeria, where the Pentecostal billboards and signposts litter their cities' skyline. Television and radio broadcasts are filled daily with competing Pentecostal churches, founders and general overseers jostling for adherents and making promises of deliverance, healings and breakthrough. In the West African context, this splintering becomes a battle for bodies and minds of people, every new assembly vying for social relevance and survival. Within the raucousness, some of these newly called and self-appointed church ministers create a fundamentalist following which is, at the same instance, proselytizing. A Jesuit theologian, Roger Haight, sees some of these movements as not only individualistic and fundamentalist, but extremely suspicious and exclusivistic of other Pentecostal assemblies. Haight avers, "so individualistic is their anthropology and piety that they scrupulously avoid all social involvement except for an extreme conservative type; and so independent and at times hostile to the interests of the mainline churches that they reject any ecumenical cooperation."[1]

Central to the thesis of this research is a critical examination of the state of ecumenism today, especially in light of the proliferation of Pentecostalism. Pentecostalism in West Africa will be used as a template for developing nations' experiences of this movement and the efforts of doing ecumenical work within Christian churches in areas such as these. Central and fundamental to this project is to question the relationship of Pentecostals with Catholicism and the already existing ecumenical unions within Christian churches. The conversation is to critically question if the arrival

1. Haight, "Responding to Fundamentalism," 60.

of Pentecostalism is a cog in the wheel of ecumenical work, or a part of the "new Pentecost" as claimed by some?

In contemporary times, it has become absolutely necessary for diverse Christian, and even religious, traditions to engage and communicate with each other through ecumenical work, which is maturing and rapidly entering into the mainstream of most societies.[2] Interreligious dialogue responds to and promotes the contemporary understanding of religious plurality, not as an issue to be remedied, but as a reality to be embraced and realized. In the face of religious fanaticism that leads to violence and accusation of proselytization, the primary goals of ecumenism are to promote interfaith understanding and encourage positive and beneficial relationships directed toward the common goal of proclaiming the good news of Jesus Christ. A good news for developing nations should lead to freedom and not to the enslavement of a people already subjugated by corrupt regimes and self-serving, self-professed religious messiahs. Jerry Pillay avers,

> The struggle for justice and peace is a very significant theological foundation for ecumenical engagement. Justice is at the heart of the gospel message . . . central theme in Jesus' preaching . . . the fulfilment of the prophetic vision of justice and other dimensions of love and grace . . . Jesus' reading from Isaiah . . . The suffering servant, with whom the church traditionally has identified Jesus, is the one who proclaims justice to the nations (Is. 42:1–4; Mt. 12:18) . . . Justice then is at the ethical core of the biblical message. Hence it is a moral imperative for Christians, especially in our time. Justice demands that we focus especially on meeting the needs of the poor, oppressed, marginalized, and excluded, both domestically and globally . . . The demand for justice permeates all social action, social relationships, and social structures. In other words, there needs to be a vision of an alternative society. Such a vision must bring with it the realization that we cannot work towards a just and peaceful society alone; we need to join with other Churches and organizations. This is what ecumenism is about.[3]

The idea of ecumenical friendship and dialogue cannot remain merely at the level of presenting a common front. Ecumenical work between churches

---

2. Johan Bonny, for instance, is of the opinion that "over the past decades there have been many favorable advances in the field of ecumenism, a shift for which we cannot but be grateful. In half a century, the relationships between Christians have been profoundly transformed across the world. The movement towards ecumenism has become an irreversible process in the Christian landscape." Bonny, "Perspectives," 108–22.

3. Pillay, "Ecumenism in Africa," 639.

Introduction

in developing nations, especially where there is unstable economic and political systems, necessarily must include a unified Christian action that strengthens and supports marginalized, disenfranchised, and oppressed peoples. Ecumenical work is not successful if the Christian communities do not act proactively on behalf of the poor. The ecumenist and Catholic priest from Tanzania, Gosbert T.M. Byamungu, states this more succinctly,

> The Church has continued to plead for justice for the poor; the documents doing so abound. What is worth pondering is the impotence of the church to transform the content of the documents into action. The "good ethos" of these good church documents has not changed the conditions of the world nor made it a better place to live in. The gap between the rich and the destitute has continued to widen. Ecumenism has not succeeded in developing dialogue beyond the level of common dogmatic understanding; more documents always remain to be produced. It is hard to implement the vision of life in common, sharing the produce of the world in common, even as we profess the same God and argue that we "belong" to the same church.[4]

Without Christians coming together in their different traditions is to deny the unifying action of the Holy Spirit in the Christian community. The same Holy Spirit vivifies the proclamation of the good news. It is this sort of unity that gives the Christian message credibility and makes for authentic and lasting conversions. According to Killian McDonnell, at a more pragmatic level, it is exactly the church's credibility that is called into question: "At the level where most persons experience the Church . . . it is the want of holiness, the lack of fruit, and the manifest disunity which make her efforts at evangelization ineffective and constitutes a threat to the power of the gospel."[5] McDonnell states further that a real commitment to Jesus consists of entering into a community of human persons totally committed to resisting popular values, "which see the ultimate goal in an ever increasing, ever higher, standard of living, of resistance to mindless consumerism, and to social values which sanction racism and the exploitation of the poor."[6] The Christian church in Africa can witness an explosion in numbers across the continent, but cannot afford in years to come to see an implosion due to present inaction. The authenticity of a true Christian spirit lies in

---

4. Byamungu, "Constructing Newer 'Windows,'" 341–52.
5. McDonnell, *Charismatic Renewal*, 16–17.
6. McDonnell, *Charismatic Renewal*, 18.

its witnessing, the power of her truth, and her forthrightness in speaking against unjust structures and domination of the poor. The appeal to divine authority, collection of tithes, promise of deliverances, revivals, night vigils, etc. may not be a veritable truth that builds real and enduring faith. If the church cannot speak this language of freedom and be at the forefront of liberation of the continent, political and economic forces will take the driver's seat. And when the dawn of a new and progressive era shines on Africa, Christianity, as we have seen on other continents, will be bagged and heaped on the garbage hill of history.

Our theological "elders" forewarned us when, in 1986, they gathered in Mexico for the Ecumenical Association of Third World Theologians (EATWOT) so that the task of Africa's theology might be ecclesial, cultural, political, and liberating. They posit the following wise words,

> we begin our common methodology of theologizing as people who feel in our bodies not just our own hearts but the pain of others. We theologize together and individually from our suffering and humiliation. We stand by our prior agreements to do theology and live our faith from the energy that flows from ecumenism and to which we pray our theology should make contribution. Together we define poverty, in the comprehensive understanding of the phenomenon, as whatever robs human beings and groups of peoples of their humanity. All who are impoverished because the culture they created has been trampled upon by others, all who's right to be human is challenged by socio-political, economic, and religious structures and demands that humiliate, all who have to struggle to have their humanity recognized and respected – all these *are poor.*[7]

It is to these poor that the good news about the kingdom of God must be preached. It is to them that the Christian church must serve and not dominate, plunder, or subjugate further than where they have already been marginalized by the corruption of governments and multimillion-dollar corporations.

All Christian churches are *Pentecostal*; they have to be since it is at Pentecost that the church was born and received the mandate and courage to evangelize. It is only through the Holy Spirit that any church can proclaim Jesus to be Lord. If the denominations then become preoccupied, exclusivist, and center on their own particular tradition, then they have

---

7. Abraham, *Third World Theologies*, 103.

Introduction

successfully marginalized the Holy Spirit. The Pentecost is deeply and theologically ecumenical as it brings different nations together and empowers them in so many languages to speak the same message of Christ. The Pentecostal nature of the Christian church then forces us to look at going beyond groupings and making the message stand, especially in opposition to the "kingdoms of this world." The churches of our time therefore must go to a place of *metanoia* and make a deep turn to truth. Put in McDonnell's words,

> Indeed, there can be no ecumenism worthy of the name without a change of heart. The merger of ecclesiastical corporations is not the goal of the ecumenical movement. It is about the reunion of penitent and reformed churches. This interior conversion demands that the full gospel be embraced, also the gospel's demand for social justice. An ecumenism which is passionately engaged in reunion efforts but is indifferent to the great social injustices does not really know what conversion is . . . action on behalf of justice and participation in the transformation of the world fully appear to . . . as a constitutive dimension of the preaching of the Gospel, or in other words, of the Church's mission for the redemption of the human race and its liberation from every oppressive situation. Ecumenism is ultimately directed to a transformed world through means of a penitent, transformed, and united church.[8]

The existing models of preaching salvation, miraculous healings, and gospels of prosperity will remain a sideshow and further collaborate in the dehumanization of a vast number of believers if the message of liberation is not included, preached, and acted upon as a fundamental option for the poor. If the various Christian communities in poor developing nations do not have a common voice against political and economic tyranny, they cannot claim to be true to the mind of Christ whose ministry rests foundationally on the idea of liberation. In the synagogue, at Jesus' self-manifestation to Israel, Jesus introduced himself and messianic message to the world, borrowing the words of the prophet Isaiah, "The Spirit of the lord God is upon me, for He has anointed me; He has sent me to bring glad tidings to the lowly, to heal the broken hearted. To proclaim liberty to captives and release to prisoners (Isa 61:1–2)." While one can presume the articulation of spiritual liberation from demonic forces as already in progress, that same claim cannot be equally made when reflecting on liberation from the evil of despotic, political, and economic oppression. Therefore, in the face of

---

8. McDonnell, *Charismatic Renewal*, 60.

a fast-growing number of Christians in developing nations, the question must be asked: what is the impact of Christian ecumenical assemblies in the face of political oppression, endemic corrupt practices in governments, the careless and relentless wasting of human lives, and the anthropological poverty of these Christians? It is situations of social and political injustices that the Christian church must first address before moving on to the sphere of eternal salvation.

This anthropological pauperization of developing nations, as Jean Mark Ela notes, was carried out to the point of paroxysm, especially in Africa. Mercy Amber Oduyoye, writing from EATWOT, notes that for the message of Christ and its uniqueness to be universal, a common methodology of theologizing in our own bodies and the pains of others must be a starting point. "We stand by our prior agreements to do theology and live our faith from the energy that flows from ecumenism and to which we pray our theology should make a contribution."[9] Oduyoye insists that to define poverty of a people comprehensively, it must be understood as whatever "robs human beings and groups of people of their humanity . . ., all who's right to be human is challenged by socio-political, economic, and religious structures and demands that humiliate, all who have to struggle to have their humanity recognized and respected."[10]

At the core of this work is the question of what ecumenical work between Catholicism and the older Christians traditions have achieved socially up till this time, then to pursue further what impact Pentecostal Christianity brings to the table within the same conversation.

The sudden demographic shift of Christianity from Western Europe to the Southern Hemisphere of Africa—and as noticed in Latin America and Asia—is a phenomenon that bestrides a transition from political self-determination by the attainment of national independence from colonization and the rapid handing over of indigenous churches from missionary hands into the service of indigenous clergies. Jerry Pillay accepts the facticity that the Global South is the new face of the growth of Christianity, but he calls for a renewed deeper and theological engagement and intentionality for African ecumenism. Pillay insists that there is a need to "shift from reactive engagements to proactive theological reading of the signs of times and speak prophetically into the context of life as we strive for a just and

---

9. Abraham, *Third World Theologies*, 103.
10. Abraham, *Third World Theologies*, 103.

Introduction

peaceful Africa and world."[11] Pillay continues, "Africans need to assess their own unique contributions to theological thinking and expressions... What have we learnt from Black Theology, African Christian Theology, African Traditional Religions, and the African Independent Churches? How do we speak to, and shape, our understanding of justice and peace and a better life for all?"[12] In a previous work, I question the validity of a Christianity that is widespread, indigenous, loud, and popular which has no recompense for the suffering masses and no rapprochement for unjust political structures thus,

> Unfortunately, in Africa, while the continent blossoms in numbers, the reality of the various nation-states is one of conflict, genocide, corruption, nepotism, sit-tight democracies that benefits only the minority ruling class at the detriment of the majority of the impoverished populace. In the face of these narratives, which are almost all pervasive on the continent, how does the blossoming of the faith impact the socio-political life of her peoples? What 'theologies' are we creating in Africa to speak to these unjust structures? Are they merely words that are theoretically thin and politically impotent? Or can we begin to build meta-narratives which are our own, about ourselves and which aims to reconstruct the future of our politics and the future of the continent? How can Africa's Christian and theological response be a proclamation and truly liberation for a disillusioned people?[13]

How does the emergence of the Pentecostal movement impact existing ecumenical work and play a role of liberation in these cultures and societies?

It is important also to examine the Pentecostal pastoral approach, which can be said to account for its upsurge. In addition, it is also important to question its truthfulness in the light of sacred Scripture and apostolic traditions to further clarify if it is a new methodology that can be adapted by the older faith traditions. And if not so, to challenge the insidious nature of characters who will manipulate others through religion for personal and selfish gains. Given the economic conditions under which many Christians survive in fledgling and developing nations, proclaiming a gospel of liberation must be seen as the task of the church and not perceived to be a tool of further oppression and subjugation. But even more importantly, this research project intends to explore how Christian churches in ecumenical

11. Pillay, "Ecumenism in Africa," 640.
12. Pillay, "Ecumenism in Africa," 640.
13. Odeyemi, "Proclamation and Liberation."

Introduction

settings such as these collaborate to empower marginalized people, streamline contextualized theology and Christian doctrine, and see as best as possible that churches are truly churches and not "incorporated" business centers.

This book is divided into six chapters with subsections. The methodology adopted is thematic so that it can be read as a whole or in sections. In chapter 1, a narrative report is given based on the data collected from the fieldwork and on both questionnaires and oral interviews. The graphs and data tools are in the glossary. In chapter 2, a historical analysis of ecumenism is delineated starting from the first council of Jerusalem through the schism of the Catholic Church of the East and the West in the eleventh century; the Reformation in the sixteenth century; the establishment of the World Council of Churches founded in 1948; the new approach of the Vatican II and its influence; and the Roman Catholic Church's involvement in ecumenism. Issues concerning the specific ecumenical relationships between Catholics and the older Christian traditions as well as the African Independent churches and the Pentecostal churches are explored. The analysis lays out broadly a history that is up-to-date for specialists and anyone interested in researching this timeline. Chapter 3 delves into the development of Pentecostalism paying particular attention to the Azusa Street movement, but making the distinction between Azusa Street and African traditional Christian Pentecostalism. This section clarifies the commonalities and differences between evangelical Pentecostals, AIC's Pentecostalism, contemporary Pentecostalism, the charismatic movement, and what I call *Pentecôtistes nouvelle génération*—newest generation Pentecostals. The immediate impact of the rising influence of Pentecostalism in West Africa on ecumenical work and its social impact are treated as part of the core questions this work seeks to respond to. In chapter 4, ecumenism in the Catholic Church from Vatican II, through the papacies of Paul VI, John Paul II, Benedict XVI, and Francis are carefully unpacked to see the consistency, or lack of, between synodal documents, papal tradition, and the magisterial tradition of the Catholic Church. In chapter 5, problems that are specific to Pentecostalism on the West African coast are marshaled out. The problems clarify some of the foundational reasons why ecumenism may not be a priority in the fast-growing assemblies and why social action is left on the backburners. Finally, in chapter 6, practical and ecclesiological problems are teased out, some pastoral recommendations are made, and a conclusion is provided.

Introduction

By the end of this research/book, I hope to have achieved a clearly articulated state of affairs of contemporary ecumenical work within Christian confessional faiths and how Pentecostalism impacts or engages these efforts. That this book is able to elucidate a clear understanding of Pentecostalism, its origin(s) historically, its various forms and persuasions, its impact, generally, but more so in economically disadvantaged nations relying on the West African experience as a paradigm for what has become a global phenomenon. Even more importantly, this book will critique ecumenism and Pentecostalism and offer, hopefully, intelligent and possible practical, pastoral, and theological solutions on improving ecumenical relationships between Pentecostals, Catholics and the rest of the Christian churches, one that especially defends the integrity of marginalized peoples.

Relying on questionnaires that were administered to founding pastors, general overseers, and congregants, I was advised to use information provided through these means mainly for data and academic purposes only. At no time will an individual pastor or church be mentioned or quoted directly. The questionnaires and interviews were carried out sampling responses from Nigeria, Ghana, Ivory Coast, and Sierra Leone. These journeys and encounters gave me an opportunity to engage first-hand in the unspoken realities of Christian associations in West Africa, which was fraught with suspicion and mistrust. Except for one occasion, the founders of mainline Pentecostal churches I attempted to interview were very difficult to reach. In some instances, especially in Nigeria and Ghana, I was given the impression that these men do not see just anybody. I witnessed first-hand, pastors who came in a motorcade of expensive, heavy-duty SUVs. To my surprise, they had armed guards and chaperones who shoved and pushed us mere earthlings away from the "man of God." In some other cases, I had to make several trips seeking appointments to speak with these pastors. The best was either to be asked politely not to return or, at the very best, to be asked to speak with a superintendent, assistant pastor, or assisting bishop. What stood out the most during the interviews and collation of questionnaires was a very clear suspicion of what the researcher intended to use the materials for. There were instances where the few assisting bishops and pastors made distinctions between their own position on a given matter, which stands in opposition to their founding father and official "church" position. This for me was a sure sign of another convinced bishop who will found another assembly—always with the claim that God told him so.

Introduction

The texts of this book will rely solely on pure empirical data and research findings. I would like to clarify that biases based on denominational affiliations do not play any role in this work. I may have the proclivity, personally, to see a united Christian church in the real sense of "one flock and one shepherd," but I am not naïve to the point of not realizing the frailty of humanity that makes this unity impossible. Reference will be made to some not-so-uplifting aspects of Pentecostalism in West Africa. They will be made only as they reflect the reality of the problems Christianity has had to endure from the apostolic era. We cannot discount the reality of these human problems and weaknesses; at the same time, we cannot overfocus on them and not see how the Holy Spirit "blows wherever it pleases," including within Pentecostalism. (The grand jury reports on Catholic priests in the State of Pennsylvania and the Cardinal McCarrick sexual abuse scandal are pointers that human weakness and sin remains within the church at all times. This makes the church home for saints and sinners, or in a more adequate sense, sinners wanting to be saints.) This is not, by any chance, polemic against the Pentecostal church or pastors. Rather, the intention is to draw out the problems that make the "new Pentecost" look more like a dividing tongue among the Christian church.

The overall hope for this work is that it shows us where we are as the body of Christ on a continent thriving in religious faith, but sadly so deficient in social justice, economic and equal opportunities for all, and the endemic problems of governance. Can we truly be "church" if we only preach and are unable to speak truth to power? Can we be truly "church" when the multitudes of believers are daily oppressed without relieve? In this work, I hope to conscientise "the new face of Christianity" in West Africa and anywhere else on the planet where people are living on the margins and the church has failed to speak and fight for them. By doing these liberating works of mercy, the kingdom of God will be established among the different nations and peoples of our world.

THE PRAYER OF JESUS FOR UNITY

And now, Father, glorify me in your presence with the glory I had with you before the world began. I have revealed you to those whom you gave me out of the world. They were yours; you gave them to me and they have obeyed your word. Now they know that everything you have given me comes from you. For I gave them the words you gave me and they accepted them. They knew with certainty that I came from you, and they believed that you sent me . . . I will remain in the world no longer, but they are still in the world and I am coming to you. Holy Father, protect them by the power of your name, the name you gave me, so that they may be one as we are one . . . They are not of the world, even as I am not of it. Sanctify them by the truth; your word is truth. As you sent me into the world, I have sent them into the world. For them I sanctify myself, that they too may be truly sanctified . . . that all of them may be one, Father, just as you are in me and I am in you. May they also be in us so that the world may believe that you have sent me. I have given them the glory that you gave me that they may be one as we are one—I in them and you in me—so that they may be brought to complete unity. Then the world will know that you sent me and have loved them even as you have loved me.

JOHN 17:5–8, 11–19, 21–23

I

Report on Fieldwork, Research Findings, and Data Analysis

Introductory Remarks

IN THE SPRING OF 2016, I applied to Missio Aachen in Germany for research funding to pursue a study of the impact of Pentecostalism on West Africa vis-à-vis the endemic poverty and political problems common in the region. This grant was given and I traveled to Ghana, Ivory Coast, Sierra Leone and Nigeria where I interviewed a good number of Pentecostal pastors, assistant bishops, and church leaders—in one instance, the founding bishop of a faith-community of Pentecostal believers. I also distributed questionnaires to lay Pentecostal congregants. Like any other researcher, fieldwork can be quite challenging because of many unforeseen circumstances and situations. However, these encounters morphed into a learning curve, revealing subtle and usually un-nuanced aspect of Christian churches' relationships. This fieldwork reveals clearly that Pentecostals and the older traditional Christian churches hold each other in mutual suspicion. As will be explicated later in this work, the factors are varied and exist on both side of the divide. This problem thus supports my initial intuition: to be aware that exploding numbers of Christians in Africa does not yet translate to "Uhuru,"[1] and having identified it as such call attention to the problem.

---

1. The word "Uhuru" is of Swahili origin and means "freedom." It has become commonplace in African writings to use this exprssion to reference completion, success, or political freedom.

Pentecostalism and Catholic Ecumenism In Developing Nations

The data collected come from two sources: questionnaires and oral interviews. (See glossary for both samples.) The questionnaires were designed for congregants and the oral interviews were originally designed to be conducted with the founders, also known in some instances as a General Overseer (GO). In some cases with the questionnaires, they were rejected because the pastors claimed that not many of the members of the church could singlehandedly answer the questions. In some other cases, questionnaires were accepted and put away, never to be distributed. And after several return visits over weeks, it became sadly clear that the questionnaires were never intended to be distributed. Out of six hundred questionnaires distributed across four West African countries: Nigeria, Ghana, Ivory Coast, and Sierra Leone, I got about 75 percent of the questionnaires back. The outcome of the questionnaires is based on about 450 responses from the four countries where the fieldwork was conducted. Data analysis revealed that about another 5–7 percent were "doctored" and could not be used in the final analysis. In the case of the oral interviews, as I already stated in the introduction to this work, I was fortunate to have a one-on-one interview with only one founding Pentecostal bishop. In every other case, I was able to interview an assistant bishop, a senior pastor, or an elder arranged to meet me. It was not always clear if the respondents were answering the questions from their own personal epistemic milieu, or they were stating their church's beliefs.

Apparently, for a little unknown researcher like me to approach the "'big man of God" was more difficult than making an effort to climb Mount Everest in the winter, or the proverbial carmel passing through the eye of the needle. There were at least two instances where I was told that research of any kind will have to be approved by the GO himself, and the waiting period to hear back was indeterminate. There were occasions where I was given the merry-go-round—"Come today, come tomorrow." After weeks, it became clear that the interview would never take place. In a particular situation, I was requested to translate my questionnaires from English to French which I did immediately through a paid translator. I submitted the questionnaires and well over two years after, not a single page has been returned. There seemed to me to be a fear, some kind of suspicion once I mentioned that I am a Catholic priest doing this research. Immediately the guard comes up, accessibility is denied. And it tells me more than the questionnaires or oral interviews that ecumenism in West Africa is only when we pray together on the World Day of Peace. Further than that,

Report on Fieldwork, Research Findings, and Data Analysis

especially regarding Pentecostal relationships with the Catholic Church in the countries I visited in West Africa, ecumenical work is almost practically nonexistent.

The questionnaires for the congregants were designed for two hundred participants in each church. I was aiming for three different churches in each country, which would have brought the questionnaires to six hundred in each country. This would have given me a wider data range for analysis. It was only in Sierra Leone that all the copies given out were returned within the time I was physical on the ground in that country. And it was administered in two Pentecostal assemblies only. Sadly, it seemed some of the questionnaires were doctored as each copy, one after the other, recorded the same responses with the same pen and handwriting. The doctored questionnaires were then not usable for the data analysis. The delay in the returns from Ghana and Nigeria set this work back for another three months. In Ghana, despite concerted efforts by my host and guide, only 180 questionnaires made it back to me. In the Ivory Coast, with all the efforts made, including paying a translator to translate from English to French, nothing came of it. Not a single copy of my questionnaires was ever returned. I gave out four hundred questionnaires between two big Pentecostal churches. Thanks to the ingenuity of my data analyst, the entire samples could have been useless.

SUMMARY: DATA ANALYSIS OF QUESTIONNAIRES

Figure 1: Distribution of survey participants by country, sex, and age group

This graph explains gender and age participation. It gives an idea of the range of converts recording a little more responses by men than women all across the board.

Table 1: Number of participants grouped by their country.

- About 50 percent of the 358 respondents are either Nigerian or males, while 15 percent are from Ghana, and 35 percent from Sierra Leone.
- About 75 percent of all respondents are between the ages of 21–70 and are working class.

Figure 2: Response on religious affiliations from birth—At and before conversion, grouped by country and gender.

The intention here was to be able to locate at which point the Pentecostal wave of conversion hit West Africa. Interestingly, the result is inconclusive enough to be able to make this connection. Broadly, researchers locate Pentecostal expansion and growth between the mid-1980s and especially in the 1990s and onwards.

- About 51 percent and 54 perecent of male and females agree that they were born Pentecostals, respectively.
- About 48 percent and 46 percent of male and females disagree that they were converted to Pentecostalism.
- The observation followed the same trend irrespective of country of the respondent.

Figure 3: Response on religious affiliations from birth—At and before conversion, grouped by country and age group.

The data gathered here is credible since it locates people born into other older traditions but later converted to Pentecostlism, and those born into Pentecostalism within the logically possible time span and brackets.

- About 56 percent of respondent less than forty years of age agree that they are Pentecostals from birth, while about 73 percent aged forty-one and above disagree. This observation followed the same trend irrespective of country of the respondent.
- About 40 percent aged less than sixty and both males and females strongly agree that Pentecostalism represents the new path to Christ. While not more than 26 percent of all respondents disagree that Pentecostalism represent the new path to Christ.

Figure 4: Previous religious affiliations before conversion grouped by country, sex, and age group. (This follows the same pattern as found above in figure 3.)

- About 65 percent of respondents between the ages of thirty-one and seventy had some form of previous religious affiliations (Catholic, Anglican, Methodist etc.), while about 80 percent of people age thirty and below had no previous religious affliation before Pentecostalism. This is significant because it locates the point at which first generation Pentecostals were born.
- About 60 percent of both male and females had no previous religious affliation before Pentecostalism
- Nigeria had the least number of respondents by percentage that had previous religious affiliation (less than 25 percent for both male and female), while Ghana had highest percentage of respondents with previous religious affiliations (59 percent male and 70 percent female). The same trend was observed for each country by age group.

Figure 5: Traditional Christian ties grouped by country and sex.

The response to this question establishes that most Pentecostals belive in the truths of the older traditions. They know that older Christian churches are authentic places of religious encounter and that all Christians have the gift of salvation. This section is interesting because it sounds almost contrary to what is heard on radio, television and on social media by some Pentecostal preachers. It is a fact that most converts to Pentecostalism were already Christians of some persuation who then were encourage to join the Pentecostal movement. Initially, the claim is made that they are invited to a Christian and non-denominational prayer group. Gradually, and by cajoling and subtly demonizing other churches, they are made into converts.

- For both males and females, majority of the respondents *disagree* that traditional churches are outdated (60 percent while 26 percent agree); Pentecostalism is the only means of a loving and personal relationship with God (50 percent disagree while 23 percent agree); only Pentecostals will be saved (68 percent disagree while 19 percent agree); and denominations should merge into one church (45.7 percent disagree while 31.7 percent agree).

Figure 6: Traditional Christian ties grouped by country and age group. (This follows the same trend as the response above in figure 5.)

However, responses from Sierra Leone seems to contradict findings from Nigeria and Ghana. A trend which I find difficult to explain or understand other than a lack of understanding of the question, or simply part of doctoring of questionnaires.

- Across age groups, the majority of respondents disagree that traditional churches are outdated, *with an average of about 60 percent.* There is no significant trend amongst the different age groups. Similarly, respondents from Ghana and Nigeria disagree that traditional churches are outdated by 74 percent and 76 percent respectively. However, a majority of the respondents (56 percent) from Sierra Leone agree that traditional churches are outdated while 32 percent disagree.

- Although there is no recognizable trend from respondents by age group, respondents from Ghana and Nigeria disagree that "Pentecostal Christianity is the only means for a loving and personal relationship with Christ," by 78 percent and 64 percent, respectively. A majority of the respondents (82 percent) from Sierra Leone agree that "Pentecostal Christianity is the only means for a loving and personal relationship with Christ," while 16 percent disagree.

- On the average across-age groups, 68 percent disagree that only Pentecostals will be saved, while 22 percent agree. By country, at least three-quarters of respondents in Ghana disagree and about half in Nigeria also disagree that only Pentecostals will be saved.

Generally, there is a 48 perecent agreement to a 46 percent disagreement that denominations should merge into one Pentecostal church. However, the older the respondents, the more likely to agree that denominations should merge into one Pentecostal church. On the flip side, Ghanaians and Nigerians tend to disagree by 74 percent to 55 percent respectively, while Sierra Leoneans agree by 82 percent.

Report on Fieldwork, Research Findings, and Data Analysis

Figure 7: Response on Christian traditions, grouped by country and sex.

These sets of questions were posed to test if the respondents have at least a minimal understanding and inclination toward a possible Christian unity. While the respondents disagree mostly on a structural merger of all Christian churches, they agree there there are historical links that bind the older and newer Christian churches and ecclesial assemblies together.

- 40 percent of the male and female respondents agree that demonimations should merge into one universal church while 38 percent disagree.
- 54 percent of the male and female respondents agree that the older Christian churches have things to teach newer Pentecostal churches while 18 percent disagree.
- 58 percent of the male and female respondents agree that there is a link between the "new Pentecost" and the Pentecost of the Acts of the Apostles while 12 percent disagree.
- 55 percent of the male and female respondents agree that there is some necessity for Christian assemblies to have a historical link to apostolic times and tradition while 24 percent disagree.

Figure 8: Response on Christian traditions grouped by country and age group. The response flows from the question or the merging of different Christian churches from charts in the glossary Figure 8.

- Generally, there is a 48 percent agreement to a 38 percent disagreement demonimations should merge into one universal church. However, the older the respondents, the more likely to agree demonimations should merge into one universal church. On the flip side, Ghanaians and Nigerians tend to disagree by 51 percent to 47 percent, respectively, while Sierra Leoneans agree by 71 percent.
- The majority (68 percent) of the respondents across all age groups and countries agree that older Christian churches have things to teach newer Pentecostal churches. At least 80 percent, 71 percent, and 63 percent of respondents from Ghana, Sierra Leone, and Nigeria agree

that older Christian churches have things to teach newer Pentecostal churches.

- About 73 percent of the respondents across all age groups and countries agree that there is a link between the "new Pentecost" and the Pentecost of the Acts of the Apostles. At least 68 percent, 88 percent, and 65 percent of respondents from Ghana, Sierra Leone and Nigeria agree that older Christian churches have things to teach newer Pentecostal churches.

- Generally, there is a 68 percent agreement that there is some necessity for Christian assemblies to have any historical link to apostolic times and tradition—the older respondents are more likely to agree. Similarly, Ghanaians, Sierra Leoneans and Nigerians tend to agree by 67 percent, 76 percent, and 62 percent, respectively.

Figure 9: Do you agree that Christian communities should play an active social role in the society? Response by country, sex, and age group.

While this question scores the highest agreement rating, it is the foundation on which both my original thesis and conclusions are grounded. We have an epistemic knowledge that the Christian churches ought to play a more important role in social and political problems across the continent, but the reality is that the churches have not responded in this manner. This section then proves that large numbers in churches, prayers tents, and rally grounds are not the entire sign that all is well either with Africa's Christianity or its Christians. Irrespective of country, sex, and age group, at least 90 percent of respondents agree that Christian communities should play an active role in the society.

Figure 10: Response on Christian ecumenism grouped by country and sex.

Again, we find a high percentage all over that agrees that ecumenism is important for Christian unity and impact on the society. The reality says otherwise. The percentages on Pentecostals being at the forefront of ecumenical work contradicts reality and previous findings. I am not particularly sure why the respondents think otherwise.

- At least 45 percent of male and female respondents agree that Christian ecumenism is necessary for all Christian churches. However, separated by country, at least 65 percent female and 70 percent male agree.
- At least 44 percent of male and 51 percent female respondents agree that Pentecostals should fully participate in ecumenical work. However, separated by country, at least 66 percent female and 70 percent male agree.
- Generally, there is a 50 percent agreement that Pentecostal Christians are already at the forefront of ecumenical efforts, with the older respondents more likely to agree. However, Ghanaians, Sierra Leoneans and Nigerians tend to agree by 54 percent, 49 percent, and 78 percent, respectively.

Figure 11: Response on Christian ecumenism grouped by country and age group:

- At least three quarters of the all the respondents agree that Christian ecumenism is necessary for all Christian churches. Separated by age group, at least 64 percent disagree while at least 69 percent agree by country.
- At least three quarters of all the respondents agree that Christian ecumenism is necessary for all Christian churches. When the data is separated by age group, at least 64 percent agree, and by country, 69 percent.
- Generally, there is a 60 percent agreement that Pentecostal Christians are already at the forefront of ecumenical efforts, with the older respondents were more likely to agree. Similarly, Ghanaians, Sierra Leoneans, and Nigerians tend to agree by 57 percent, 77 percent, and 49 percent, respectively.

Questionnaires are not altogether dependable for various reasons. In this instance, there is no yardstick in judging how educated respondents are. There is no guarantee that they fully understand the questions or tease out the interconnectedness of the questions. There is also no guarantee that some questionnaires were either doctored—just randomly marking the options—or that some were tutored—where a group got together and a leader told them what to mark. Whatever the case might be, the data generated from these questionnaires provides enough grounds to base this work's fundamental assumptions.

ANALYSIS OF ORAL INTERVIEWS

The fieldwork for this project was done in two months, covering Ghana, Ivory Coast, Sierra Leone, and Nigeria, in this order. There were some problems encountered in trying to carry out oral interviews which are worthy of note. First, it was extremely difficult to make contact with the leadership of most Pentecostal churches. Whenever contact was eventually made, anonymity was required before an appointment was set up for the interview. It was very clear that being introduced as a Catholic priest made people uneasy. Unfortunately, it was thereafter difficult to explain that I was simply conducting a research. It became abundantly clear to me that ecumenical work between neo-Pentecostalism and other older Christian churches, perhaps Catholicism is more suspect, will continue to be a problem to overcome. The bigger and successful Pentecostal ministries, especially in Nigeria and Ghana, were the most difficult to reach. The overall head was treated more or less like celebrity rock star. In a particular Pentecostal church in Lagos, the secretary looked at me incredulously, struggling not to ask me if I was out of my mind for having the audacity to want to speak with the big man of God. Whether in the traditional and older Christian churches, or the newer Christian movements, servants of the gospel should not deviate from the simple and humble lifestyle of the carpenter from Galilee. In another Pentecostal church in Ivory Coast, I was told that it is the policy of the church not to give out interviews or accept questionnaires of any sorts.

Following directly below is a summary of my transcription of the responses from people who were interviewed. Since anonymity was requested, I cannot use names of interviewee or use the name of their churches. I also decided to condense the responses into one as much as they are in agreement. And where the answers defer, I will state the differentiation. I was able to interview a founding archbishop, a junior Bishop, and two associate pastors. All tapes are kept as records of the interviews. I have also had to condense the responses for the sake of brevity. Sometimes, the discussions went in different directions and it was difficult to rein in the speaker and get them back on point.

PASTORS'/GO'S QUESTIONNAIRE

What are the factor(s) that led you to a personal call to found a church/Christian community?

There is an interesting and common thread in all of the separate interviews granted. The corollaries found include the fact that all of these men encountered Pentecostalism while at the university. All of them can be considered first generation Pentecostals. They were born into an older Christian tradition before they were converted in the University through the evangelical work of the Scripture Union (SU). They are graduates in professional fields: one in chemical engineering, another in business studies, one in political science, and another in agricultural studies. Two were directly influenced by the charismatic founder and leader of the Pentecostal church they currently work for. The others were influenced indirectly. All of them perceive a call like the apostles in the Scriptures—called from what is familiar to this new life in ministry, called from the world to be born-again. Interestingly, all of them used the expression to explain their "vocation" as "the great commission." Quoting Matthew 28:18–19, "Go therefore make disciples of all nations." They all believe that their founding pastors were specially called by God to lead a new way of experiencing God in the Holy Spirit. One person pointed out the huge success of the founding pastor's ministry as proof of God's approval and seal. The great commission came about because of a need for renewed evangelism, which is beginning to bear great fruits in the growing number of born-again Christians across the continent.

In the light of this call/vocation, how do you respond to and understand Jesus' prayer for the unity of his body in John's Gospel? (John 17:20–23)

The general response to question too reads off of a current ecumenical script: the understanding and personal translation that the prayer of Jesus did not imply one united and universal church. Rather, they understand this prayer for a "united Christian body in the profession of a living faith in

Christ and in His words." Even when I pointed out that the prayer seemed to invite others who were outside inside the fold, it seems difficult to comprehend since, apparently, they are in the fold, and it looks like the older traditions are outside the fold. This is not stated specifically but it is made easy to deduce. One respondent likened his coming into the Pentecostal church from the Methodist church (where his father is and remains a member) as coming from darkness into the light.

In which ways do you understand Christian ecumenical efforts?

The responses are very similar: the respondents all understand and perceive Christian ecumenical work from the standpoint of common pushback against government policies that alienate Christians, or as a reaction to extreme and fundamentalist Islamic insurgencies. Each country has an established ecumenical body and another arm of Pentecostal fellowship. Within these various groups, there are more problems than there are issues of unity. In most cases, coming together depends on the exigent needs of the moment, and after the issues are resolved, everyone returns to their familiar camps.

Do you see any necessity for ecumenical work among the various churches?

There is a common response that there is a need for ecumenical work among various Christian churches, but there is also a common ground that we are yet to arrive at a real and full realization of this ideal.

In what ways do you think dialogue within the churches should proceed and what objectives should they strive to achieve?

Each respondent proffered that for true dialogue to lead to any meaningful unity, the first thing to overcome are inherent problems. They cite mistrust, demonization of each other, personal interest in increasing followership which leads to proselytization, and the arrogance by which the older traditional churches look down on the newer movements. They argue that mutual respect and acceptance will go a long way to bring everyone together and build a formidable Christian community made of many denominations/churches.

What do you perceive to be the reason(s) for the division(s) that sets Pentecostalism apart from the older Christian traditions?

With reasons given in the previous section, research finds that they added that Pentecostals and the older traditions do not get along because, while the Pentecostals are vibrant and expressive in their worship, the older churches remain somber in line with their colonial and European antecedents. It was suggested by one respondent, an assistant bishop, that the Pentecostal movement is the new phase of the church going forward. He opines that the older traditions have fulfilled their mission, and the next phase of the development of the church is a Holy Spirit-led community, patterned after the church of the apostles. They will be the new evangelizers, the new way of being an ecclesial community and bring many more to Christ.

What do you suppose are the attractions of Pentecostalism which account for its current appeal and numerical strength?

Vibrancy of worship, Holy Spirit inspired teachings, and the experience of "gifts" of the Holy Spirit are the leading attractions. Followed by the fact that the style of worship is not a strictly formalized and strictly adhered to liturgy, it is therefore "user-friendly," and attractive to an African's mind. The link to the vibrancy of African worship vis-à-vis Pentecostal worship connects to the idea of battling the dark forces of the spiritual world, setting people free from ancestral curses, the power of witches and wizards, demonic forces, and machination of envious neighbors and co-workers. Added to these are prayers for financial breakthrough, success in business or advancement by promotion at jobs, opening and begetting the "fruit of the womb," success in exams, securing a life partner, and even the securing of traveling visa documents. These miracles attract people to the Pentecostal assemblies as it assuages the disappointment, mostly in a public system that has failed and does not provide a safety net for the welfare of its people.

Pentecostalism and Catholic Ecumenism In Developing Nations

What would you consider the basic foundations of Pentecostal evangelism, mission, and ministry?

Two models were introduced which have very clearly set out patterns for evangelism, mission, and ministry. First, there is the application of what is called the 3 *Rs*: reaching out, reaching in, and releasing. Second, evangelizing, witnessing, and teaching leading to freedom. There is a common thread that reflects on "the great commission": Jesus' call to go out into the whole world and make disciples of all nations taken from Matthew 28:19–20. There is an acknowledgement that, in terms of evangelizing in areas yet un-evangelized, the Pentecostal church has not made any significant impact in this area. The end to which all of this is directed is to win souls for Christ and bring people to the kingdom of God.

How do Pentecostals understand authority, clerical order, and discipline in its governing structure?

The idea of hierarchical structure and clerical discipline is mostly at infancy level. The respondents I interviewed belong to communities where the founding father is alive and in charge. One founding bishop is aware of the necessity to put a structure in place; therefore, he established a board of trustee who will be responsible for running the church after his retirement or demise. A bishop in another Pentecostal church enumerated what could be considered a well-charted organogram of governing structure for the church. They have a directorate chaired by the founding father, a board of trustees, a national executive council made of presiding pastors, mummy (founding father's wife), senior pastors at state and parish levels, as well as in the diaspora, and then church council. They also have a national association of pastors' directorate where issues of mission, pastoral work, training, administration, and finance are handled. On the question of clerical discipline, it is clear that mostly, things are still at the level of "make it up as you go." From responses, it is still very much at the level of fraternal corrections, possible suspension, or demotion before considering an outright sack or expulsion. Unfortunately, once in a while, when an expulsion has been handed out, the pastor in question leaves and starts his own church, multiplying further an already fragmented Pentecostal church.

Report on Fieldwork, Research Findings, and Data Analysis

Do you think Pentecostalism is a passing phenomenon, as some say, or a "new Pentecost" and renewal of the churches into the future?

Except for the one respondent who argues that the Pentecostal assembly is the next phase of the Christian church, the others argue for, first, different traditions co-existing and giving different people an opportunity to find where they belong. Second, the Pentecostal church challenges the older tradition, but to make any other claims about the future of the bride of Christ is not legitimate. Third, and lastly, for a church to continue to endure, it must make the gospel its fundamental message and core project. However, the respondents point out the sweeping reforms in the ecclesial life of the older Christian traditions since the charismatic movements started in them. They believe this came about based on the challenges brought through Pentecostalism. And since it is the same Spirit that is the driving force of both the charismatic and Pentecostal life, then the churches in their tradition will endure.

In conclusion, I had the opportunity to attend various Pentecostal services in all four countries. It is easy to see how fervent the people are in their faith and trust in God. I focused on the style of worship and the content of the preaching. While the older traditions, in prayers, seek a connection with the divine in the self, the Pentecostals seek it in an explosion outside of the self. While the older traditions adhere to a strictly outlined liturgy, the Pentecostals are flexible and more malleable and are "open" to the directions of the Holy Spirit. In terms of preaching, the older Christian churches are often more tactile in theological applications and exegetical application of scriptural texts. However, Pentecostal preachers seem more likely to approach scriptural interpretation mostly from an allegorical and eisegetical perspective as long as it supports the message of the day. Also, in the bigger and more successful Pentecostal assemblies, the preaching is oftentimes motivational speaking or even business classes. The teaching of preaching addresses mostly how to be successful in a competitive world of commerce and industry. Whatever the case might be, like the rest of the Christian churches, they pray together, and encourage and support each other, thereby creating new ecclesial community of brethren. Since they gather in the name of Jesus, then the Lord himself is there in their midst, as he is in other Christian communities too.

It is well known that Pentecost reverses Babel. The people who built the tower of Babel sought to make a name, and a unity, for themselves. At Pentecost, God builds his temple, uniting people in Christ. Unity—interpretive agreement and mutual understanding—is, it would appear, something that only God can accomplish, and accomplish it he does, but not in the way we might have expected. Although onlookers thought that the believers who received the Spirit at Pentecost were babbling (Acts 2:13), in fact they were speaking intelligibly in several languages (Acts 2:8–11). Note well: they were all saying the same thing (testifying about Jesus) in different languages. It takes a thousand tongues to say and sing our great Redeemer's praise. Protestant evangelicalism evidences a Pentecostal plurality: the various Protestant streams testify to Jesus in their own vocabularies, and it takes many languages (i.e. interpretive traditions) to minister the meaning of God's Word and the fullness of Christ. As the body is made up of many members, so many interpretations may be needed to do justice to the body of the biblical text. Why else are there four Gospels, but that the one story of Jesus was too rich to be told from one perspective only? Could it be that the various Protestant traditions function similarly as witnesses who testify to the same Jesus from different situations and perspectives?"

—Kevin J. Vanhoozer

2

Ecumenism

ECUMENISM IN A NATURAL sense has existed in Christian antiquity from the early church of the apostles. While it is not necessarily what it is today, the idea of presenting a common front while stating the doctrinal position of the church is a common thread. The first council of Jerusalem, while debating circumcision either as a necessity or not, for gentile converts to be admitted into the Christian community, unknowingly, engaged in ecumenical work.[1] Earlier on, confronted with the question of care for Jewish and Hellenist widows, the apostles conferred and made the decision, through the Holy Spirit, to create the office of the diaconate. This office of service was to relieve the apostles and not hinder the preeminent task of proclaiming the good news.[2]

Professor G.O. Abe draws our attention to a pre-existing idea of ecumenism in the Old Testament as championed by the prophets and Israel's Yahwism. According to Abe, the universal scope of Israel's worship of Yahweh exists within an ecumenical scope from the inception of Israel's faith, through pre- and post-exilic intertestamental periods; Yahweh-Elohim as universal Lord and creator rules over the entire peoples/nations of the world, and all the peoples should in unity and common faith acknowledge and worship him. In the prophetic vocations of Ezekiel, Jeremiah, Isaiah and the other prophets, Israel's apostasy is called into question with a constant call for a restored community. For instance, "Ezekiel advocated

---

1. Acts 15:1–35.
2. Acts 6:1–7.

a theocratic community, a temple centered society in which all the nations would bring offering to Yahweh and engage in his worship. His ideal was an ecclesiastical community of ecumenical relations."[3] Post exilic Judaism produced various sects to sustain and order Judaism: the strict Orthodox Pharisees who were scribes of the law, the Sadducees who were born of the aristocratic and wealthy high priestly families, and the Essenes were also of the priestly family and lived in community. All of these groups preserved the Judaic rites in an "ecumenical spirit, based on the prophetic emphasis that with the restoration of the Jews all nations would come to recognize the superiority of Yahweh over the universe."[4]

Subsequently, in the New Testament and apostolic church, debates over doctrine and the profession of the faith continued. It was not until the schism that rocked the early church in the eleventh century created the separation between the Catholic Church of the East and the West that the seriousness of these disagreement's impact was felt with full force. Some of the issues causing dissension among the various early communities include authority in the church, the definition of doctrines, and proper and authoritative interpretation of Scriptures and jurisdiction. The Reformation in the sixteenth century remains another major dislocation and stumbling block which greater ecumenical work to date is still trying to heal the wounds of its division. Mark Lowery expounds further that the complexities of the division of both eras include other factors, "theological, political, socioeconomic, and psychological. Added to this intricate interplay was the fact that opposing parties were simply unwilling to openly dialogue with each other."[5] Deji Ayegboyin makes an important point when he averred that in cases such as this in the African context, there are some other specific problems hindering the success of ecumenical work from the very beginning,

> The reformation ... coupled with the great Awakening/Evangelical Revival Movements, resulted in the founding of missionary bodies and denominations, some of which evangelized Africa. These bodies, even though seemed to have the same goal, presented the gospel to Africa as dictated from "home." And so we have replicated in Africa a Church that was fragmented right from its inception.[6]

---

3. Ishola and Ayegboyin, *Rediscovering and Fostering*, 54.
4. Ishola and Ayegboyin, *Rediscovering and Fostering*, 54.
5. Lowery, *Ecumenism*, 12.
6. Ishola and Ayegboyin, *Rediscovering and Fostering*, 18.

Ecumenism

It was not until the creation of the World Council of Churches (WCC) in 1948 that the Christian church seemed to become more alert to the necessity for ecumenical cooperation. At the inauguration of the WCC in Amsterdam in 1948, 148 churches from 44 countries attended their first general assembly. In 1954, the second general assembly was held in Evanston, Illinois, USA, and the third assembly in 1961 was held in New Delhi, India. It recorded 625 official delegates in attendance and 175 churches participating, this time including some observers from the Catholic Church. By the fourth general assembly held in Upsala, Sweden in 1968, a consensus had been reached that the WCC is "a fellowship of Churches which confess Jesus as Lord and savior according to scriptures, and therefore seek to fulfil together their common calling to the glory of the one God, Father, Son and the Holy Spirit."[7] The WCC makes it clear that it does not represent a super church, but places itself at the service of all 220 member churches.[8]

Since Vatican II, there has been a renewed interest in ecumenical work spearheaded by the Catholic Church. While no one can lay claim to any kind of structural unity, a peaceful, albeit fraternal, communion in dialogue now exists. In most places, this effort includes ecclesial non-denominational worship, dialogue, and even liturgical communion services. From all practical experience, it seems ecumenism has come to settle for a peaceful co-existence and the toleration of a fragmented Christianity. Sadly, this state of affairs makes the possibility of presenting a cohesive message of the good news and witness to a secularized world difficult, if not totally estranging Christianity from an unbelieving world. The context and space in which ecumenical work must be done is now totally different from the Renaissance, the Enlightenment, Scientific Revolution, or post-modernity. The challenges of technology, globalization, and secularism present a new cultural dynamism which challenges the Christian churches to a crucial cohesiveness in presenting a unified vision of the gospel message to a new world. There are also newer and more contemporary scientific and ethical debates that often stand at odds with the Christian message, which needs a Christian answer. We have witnessed in history, the conflict between political and economic policies which directly opposes basic Christian ethical principles and practices. While the uniqueness of each faith confessing communities remains, lack of unity in confession continually hinders

---

7. Rahner, Ernst, and Smyth, *Sacramentum Mundi*, 192–94

8. In this paragraph, I relied mostly on facts and figures from Rahner, Ernst, and Smyth's *Sacramentum Mundi*.

ecumenical work and the possibility of a unified response to some excessiveness of liberalized post-modern moral, social, economic, political, and cultural changes.

Ecumenism bridges the gap that the Christian church has created by the emergence of a myriad of diverse traditions springing forth from the same traditional roots of the apostolic church. These divergent traditions came about as a result of disagreement over how to carry on transmitting Christian traditions and apply them to the ever-changing social landscape of humanity's cultures and historical epochs. Unable to proffer a uniform approach, a pluriform presentation of doctrinal development of various traditions became necessary. According to Mark D. Lowery, to view ecumenism in these divergent traditions, "unity does not imply uniformity."[9] Lowery states further, "Pluralism or pluriformity implies that one particular approach to God is not necessarily the only good approach."[10] The challenge now in history was to overcome the bitter rivalry and animosity that, centuries after the Reformation, had existed between Catholics and Protestants. The Reformation gave birth to Catholics' Counter-Reformation, which for about four centuries was marked by apologetics and polemics, each side arguing and countering arguments about who was right and who was wrong. These were "dark ages" in Christian fellowship which ecumenism wished to respond to and call the churches to renewal and conversion.

Etymologically, ecumenism is generally understood to come from a Greco-Roman politically created word that expressed the superiority and conquest of the Greek and Roman civilizations and created them as superpowers of their time. *Oukoimene* is derived from the Greek, meaning the inhabited world. Derived from a feminine gender, *o'ikos* gives a sense of filial relationship based on a common maternity. When the word is adapted in English to ecumenism, it "refers to the inhabitants of the earth, the whole world or human race or mankind."[11] In popular usage, it "covers the search for Christian unity achieved through theological study, common testimony for the benefit of the universal task of the mission and evangelism, as well as through the promotion of justice and peace."[12] Within the Catholic Church, it refers to the various general councils of the Church worldwide—closest

---

9. Lowery, *Ecumenism*, 17.
10. Lowery, *Ecumenism*, 17.
11. Ishola and Ayegboyin, *Rediscovering and Fostering*, 50
12. Brie, "Contemporary Ecumenism," 260.

Ecumenism

to modern times are Vatican Councils I[13] and II.[14] According to Mircea Brie, contemporary ecumenical efforts can be divided into three epochs: from the mid-nineteenth century to the beginning of the twentieth century as the starting point. The first half of the twentieth century gave birth to interconfessional and intercontinental movement working to present Christian message in unity. Third, and lastly, from 1950, ecumenical work has become a more conscientious task of the various churches.[15] Brie notes, however, that ecumenical work and development also has had its fair share of problems and suspicions:

> It is a known fact that ecumenism is regarded with suspicion in particular milieus of the churches participating in the dialogue. The advocates of the anti-ecumenical way of thinking fear that the ecumenical movement can degenerate into a pietistic sentimentalism, irresponsible in relation to doctrine, or into syncretic metaconfessional utopia, or, further still, into a pan humanistic ideology, which is based on an egalitarian philanthropic concept, or even into a transactionist ethos, according to which the truth of faith is relativized into a "human family" lacking any distinctive profile. In such circumstances, ecumenism becomes the problem rather than the solution: it leads neither to Christian unity, nor does it allow the followers of Jesus to discuss honestly about some issues which cannot be turned into the object of political "negotiations."[16]

Brie's assertion supports many of my findings across the four countries along the West African coastline where my fieldwork was conducted.[17] Various Christian associations and ecumenical bodies are heavily politicized and oftentimes are in cahoots with corrupt government officials, thereby turning leadership positions in these bodies into highly coveted positions to hobnob with politicians and those in the corridors of power.

---

13. Held in Rome from 1869–1870 and convened by Pope Pius IX in 1864. It was the twentieth ecumenical council of the Catholic Church with a central focus on the definition of Papal infallibility

14. The second Vatican Council was convened by Pope John XXIII in January 1959, but held from 1962–1965. It was the twenty-first ecumenical council of the Catholic Church. It aimed at a spiritual renewal of the church and an invitation to separated Christians to join in ecumenical work for Christian unity.

15. Brie, "Contemporary Ecumenism," 261.

16. Brie, "Contemporary Ecumenism," 262.

17. See the section on the report of fieldwork in chapter 1.

Other major obstacles will be reviewed more expansively later on in chapter 5 of this work.

In places where there is evidence of some level of friendliness among churches, while the segregated autonomy of churches remains, the borders have become more porous and permeable. In most cases in West Africa, close family ties and social ties force interfaith celebrations. Oftentimes, weddings, funerals, and thanksgiving services make cross-carpeting a non-issue. With the advent of Pentecostalism and the various campgrounds and revivals, forces of demonic oppression, economic bondage, and deliverances and healings (sometimes labelled non-denominational events), the borders are wide open and people easily crisscross. Sadly, for the conditions in West Africa, these events do not constitute any kind of efforts at ecumenism of the churches. It is much more a signifier of attempts at proselytizing. Even though these events are at least non-violent and afford Christians to enter into worship together, they fail, woefully, if the WCC's ratified charter is right where it states,

> The unity of the church to which we are called is a koinonia given and expressed in the common confession of the apostolic faith; a common sacramental life entered by the one baptism and celebrated together in one Eucharistic fellowship; a common life in which members and ministries are mutually recognized and reconciled; and a common mission witnessing to the gospel of God's grace to all people and serving the whole creation.[18]

For those who think these acts of common worship are all that is needed, ecumenism has failed and died a natural death. The ordinary person who is not bothered about arguments and apologetics is not concerned about ecumenism. Michael Root, in his work states, "the tentative conclusion can be reached that one aspect of the stagnation that seems to beset contemporary ecumenism stems from a widespread (but not universal) sense that the present situation represents all that is really to be desired."[19] Yet, the onus is on the Christian church to keep this flame of ecumenism burning. Killian McDonnell calls attention to the fact that "division of the church is in scandalous opposition to the declared will of Christ, a painful, sinful fact, with which Christianity cannot become comfortable."[20]

---

18. Kinnamon, *Signs of Spirit*, 173.
19. Root, "Unity of Church," 390.
20. McDonnell, *Charismatic Renewal*, 62.

It is worthwhile to take a brief excursion into the history of ecumenism. This is to provide a background for readers who may not be familiar with this field. There are works in abundance that thematically give a concise and clear chronology of events in this field. Here, with broad strokes, I will present an account that is easy to grasp and understand. It is also important to note that the Reformation will play a big role several centuries later in the missionary activities of the different denominations, especially in Africa, thereby sowing seeds of discord and disunity among the young Christian churches as they grew from missionary enterprise. This is clearly seen especially in the southwestern parts of Nigeria where certain regions are clearly of one denomination than another.

SCHISMS/REFORMATION: THE CHURCHES OF THE EAST AND THE WEST

There have been numerous schisms and schismatics in the history of Christianity down through the ages. A schism happens when there is a break, dissention, or willful separation from ecclesiastical communion and unity. In the classical ecclesiology of Roman Catholicism, schism is understood as holding a divergent opinion from the magisterium of the church or to cause a rupture in the communion with the Petrine see. A distinction is thus clearly designated; schism can be understood from two perspectives: "canonically, it signifies a breach in jurisdictional relations with the see of Rome... theologically, schism is understood to place an obstacle to the full and manifest realization of unity in faith and participation in the church as the one, unique, sacramental and hierarchical reality."[21]

Schisms, particularly between the East and the West and the Reformation, gave new vitality to the idea of modern ecumenism. The New Dictionary of Theology states it quite clearly thus,

> In the contemporary ecumenical climate, Roman Catholic theology believes that it is possible within history to achieve a truly universal unity which is both spiritual and visible. It does not reserve the achievement of this unity to an ultimate eschatological fulfilment. This is because the kingdom of God has already begun and moves forward in history to its full manifestation... The healing of schisms is at the center of the ecumenical movement. This healing takes different forms. For some Protestant communities, it

21. Komonchak, Collins, and Lane, *New Dictionary*, 934.

takes the form of mutual agreements in the practice of intercommunion, pulpit sharing and other aspects of worship without necessarily achieving full agreement on matters of doctrine. Others, who fall under the general category "Catholic," seek unanimity of faith and agreement with regard to the hierarchical sacramental structure first before engaging in full sacramental communion.[22]

Schisms are an unusual occurrence in modern times, but in a technical sense, some recently found that churches and their leaders can be considered schismatics if understood from the perspective of an inability to articulate properly beliefs, which are in consonance with general Christian doctrinal and creedal professions. The proliferation of the Christian church, especially with the Pentecostal deluge in developing nations, calls our attention to a necessary reevaluation of ecumenical work.

Ecumenical gatherings started with the growth and expansion of the early church, especially within the five patriarchates: Jerusalem, Rome, Alexandria, Antioch and Constantinople. These patriarchates will split between the Latin/Western rite church in Rome with the Pope, bishop of Rome as its head, and the Eastern/Greek rite church with patriarchs heading each patriarchate. As the churches grew, there was the necessity again, just like the church of the apostles already mentioned, to harmonize beliefs, teachings, and Christian tradition. To successfully do this, the bishops from the fourth and fifth centuries started to hold what is known as ecumenical councils. What has now become commonly referred to as East-West Schism came to a head by the Council of Chalcedon in 451 AD. Here, Rome rejected according major jurisdictional powers to the Patriarchate of Constantinople. Following closely behind, at the third Council of Constantinople in 680 AD, the disagreement on monothelitism, the argument that there is only one divine will in Christ, this schism, according to Richard McBrien, escalated over a considerable number of years with various political and theological misunderstandings between the East and the West, exacerbating an already tense relationship. The final straw was the crusade of 1202–1204 in which the crusaders sacked Constantinople without sparing even churches. Despite various efforts at reconciliation, notably in 1276 at the Council of Lyons, and in 1439 at Council of Florence, none were able to broker a lasting resolution. It was not until 1965, when the Pope John XXIII convened Second Vatican Council, on December 7, Pope Paul

---

22. Komonchak et al., *New Dictionary*, 935.

VI and Patriarch Athenagoras mutually lifted anathemas imposed by both sides since 1054.[23]

Ecumenical work currently continues to move away from doctrinal controversies, which has been its dog-eared history. The shift now is an attempt not only to present a unified voice in the face of oppression or injustice, but also to work together for welfare, relief, and social service for people who are displaced or disadvantaged. This has not been by any chance an easy task. The ideological and religious division between the West and the East has created a Catholic-Protestant Western Christianity as against Eastern Orthodox Christian Churches. Unfortunately, both blocks are now facing a greater threat in the expansionism and dangers of radical-extreme Islam. We can no longer completely ignore ecumenical work, but must also pay attention to interreligious dialogues.

THE REFORMATION

The Reformation of the Christian church in the sixteenth century, contrary to what oftentimes is wrongly placed solely at Martin Luther's door, was an event that was precipitated by various social forces, as well as political, intellectual, cultural, and religious factors. Major events which culminated in the Reformation are a plethora of events. They include the corruption of the papacy, a disconnection between theology and piety—also between theology and the biblical tradition of the church—a new humanism embodied in the Renaissance, and a turning away from Scholasticism. A subtle but very real after-effect of the Western schism was the beginning of nation-states and the rejection of the Catholic Church's role in politics, as well as a rise in anti-clericalism that was not devoid of the impact of Western civilization. More importantly, the impact of the reformers Martin Luther, Ulrich Zwingli and John Calvin was a result.

Luther's spiritual journey as a monk led him to a personal reawakening which gave him subjective insights into the perturbing question about the last things (parousia). He also became acutely disturbed by what he perceived to be excess in an overly clericalized and corrupt church. It all came to a head on October 31, 1517 when he posted his now famous ninety-five theses on the door of the church in Wittenberg. Arguments abound as to Luther's overall intentions, but I think it is right to assume that Luther himself could not have foreseen the extent to which his actions would change

23. McBrien, *Catholicism*, 625–27.

Pentecostalism and Catholic Ecumenism In Developing Nations

the course of the Christian Church's world history. Some commentators suggest that if Luther had not stood his ground at the Diet of Worms,[24] where he was given the opportunity to recant, that there probably would have not been such events as the French Revolution, the modern societal idea of freedom in the West, or America as we know it. Luther's reaction was the trigger by which Henry VIII caused the breakaway between the Catholic Church and what became the Church of England. Henry VIII's saga of divorce and remarriage was only possible if he operated outside of Catholicism and papal authority. Luther and the events in history at the time gave the perfect grounds by which schism and fracture could occur. In a certain sense, Luther's hope of an internal reform of the church became a veritable tool in the hands of the landowners, aristocrats, and dissenting monarchies.

Zwingli's form of Protestant Reformation took some steps forward beyond Luther. He turned totally away from the ecclesiology of the Catholic Church. He preached what he called the early primitive church without the Roman influence. This was a church in which clericalism had no place, a church that, as an institution, was converted to a lay government running the affairs of the church in a democratic setting. On the other hand, Calvin is seen to be the moderate of the extreme right of Luther and extreme left of Zwingli. It is argued that he was moderate to the Catholic-ness still found in Luther, who held on to the crucifix, and Zwingli, who abolished in totality any kind of images including the cross. Calvin[25] accepted a cross

---

24. Diet of Worms was the assembly held on April 18, 1521 in Germany. The Holy Roman Emperor, Charles V, invited Luther to recant from the charges of heresy which he faced. Luther remained adamant and, in some ways, this was pivotal to the Protestant Reformation.

25. There are quite a few scholars in American academia who argue that Calvin was more interested in a Reformation of the Roman Church than the break and separation it resulted into. According to Randal Zachman, theologian and specialist in Reformation studies out of the University of Chicago, "First of all, it is an acknowledgement that Calvin did not envision himself as the founder of a new tradition called 'Calvinism,' but rather as one who sought to restore the Catholic Church to what he called its 'purer form' under the apostles and early Church writers. Calvin thought of himself as belonging to the 'orthodox and evangelical' tradition, which associated him not only with Martin Luther, Philipp Melanchthon, Martin Bucer, and Heinrich Bullinger, but also with Cyprian, Ambrose, Chrysostom, and Augustine . . . his desire to restore the Catholic Church of his day, Calvin's engagement with is contemporary Roman Catholics was not tangential to his concerns, but was directly related to the task he was called to carry out. By placing Calving and his followers within the context of their wider interactions with Roman Catholics . . . we can gather a better grasp of what the real issues were that both

Ecumenism

without the corpus on it. His approach was more systematic theologically. His establishment of *The Institute of the Christian Religion* in 1536 and profession of predestination as a central belief made Calvinism the face of the Protestant Reformation. The Anabaptists and Anglicans also played important roles in the Reformation. The Anabaptists went further left even of Zwingli. They disagreed with the Catholic baptism of infants, arguing that baptism must be for convinced and converted persons. This earned them the name "Anabaptist," meaning baptized again. The Anglicans born of religious upheavals and English nationalism went far right beyond even Luther. Anglicanism was borne out of a showdown between Henry VIII and Pope Clement VII. Henry VIII, in order to divorce his wife and remarry in the church, accepted Protestantism and usurped the church in England. This remains the singular reason why the English monarch is also the head of the Church of England.[26]

I find the following summary from the *Oxford History of Christianity* a concise example of the situation surrounding the Reformation of the sixteenth century. It states:

> But the reformation was more than politics, more even than ecclesiastical politics. If it is to be explained pathologically, in terms of a *malaise*, then the *malaise* was more deep-seated, spiritual as well as institutional. If, on the contrary, it is understood as an episode of renewal and reconstruction, then it has to be described as a religious revival involving new teaching, new certainties, a new and transforming spirit which drew its strength from the very past which it repudiated. Negatively, the reformation entailed various versions of anticlericalism, the urge to reduce the role in society of the clergy and to place limits on the space which priests and other religious persons occupied and the privileges and material rewards which they enjoyed, above all their capacity to overrule the laity. The other side of this coin was the assertion of the glorious liberty of the sons of God, all the sons, summed up in the figure identified by Luther as 'the Christian man' (and, in somewhat smaller print, the Christian woman).[27]

---

united and divided them, and we will be able to see more clearly how members of the old church regarded the work of Calvin and his colleagues . . . It is not possible to study the Reformed and Roman Catholic communities in isolation from each other . . . Protestantism and Catholicism cannot be fully understood in isolation from each other." Zachman, *John Calvin*, 9–10.

26. McBrien, *Catholicism*, 635.

27. McManners, *Oxford Illustrated History*, 237–38.

Pentecostalism and Catholic Ecumenism In Developing Nations

The Reformation marks a watershed in the history of the Christian church. Prior to this event, the schism in the church created one church, separated geographically as East and West, that had the same creedal formula and doctrinal differences that could be overlooked. The main issue for resolution remained on the question of primacy between the see of Rome and the patriarchates of the East. The Reformation and all of its attendant exigencies colluded to create a fragmented universal Christian church. And centuries after, the churches of different places are still trying to mop up the mess made in the sixteenth century by all the major actors of the time, including the overbearing and excessive powermongering of the Roman church of that era.[28] Thanks to the Reformation, it is the reason for the necessity for ecumenical work.

---

28. The foregoing forms a theological and historical background to understanding the difference and classification of the reason(s) for the separation from the schism to the Reformation, and to note carefully the difference between that on the further fragmentations afterwards. Bernard Leeming in his works notes, "The obstacles are not everywhere the same, but differ mainly according to the history and the nationality of the various groups . . . These Churches have certain great advantages when compared with the various groups that cut themselves off in the sixteenth century. The Orthodox Churches have preserved unbroken the succession of their bishops from the apostles and, along with that, valid sacraments, above all, the Eucharist. In doctrine they retain the ancient apostolic and patristic tradition, and differ from the faith of the Latin Church only in a few points, particularly in their denial of the dogmas defined by Councils since their separation, such as the primacy and infallibility of the Roman Pontiff. Although they have not accepted the definitions of the Immaculate Conception and the Assumption, devotion to the blessed virgin remains strong among them, and the substance of these dogmas can be found in their liturgical books and is generally accepted by their faithful. Objection to them lies mainly in their definition after the breach with Rome.

In the course of the centuries, however, the concept of the unity of the Church among these churches has changed. According to the doctrine that prevails among Orthodoxy today, this unity does not demand the subordination and submission of each single church or group of churches to a single head, who will be the successor of Peter, the Vicar of Christ, the Roman Pontiff. Rather, they say, it is established by the mutual 'communion' of the individual local church, that is, by agreement in faith and in the 'mysteries' (sacraments) and in certain feeling of brotherhood. The individual churches do not recognize among themselves a head that would have authority over all." Bea, *Unity of Christians*, 41.

ROMAN CATHOLICS, AICS, PENTECOSTALS RELATIONSHIPS

From my experience and fieldwork in West Africa, the relationship between Catholics, African Independent Churches (AICs) and the Pentecostals in ecumenical work is not easily navigated. It is different from one socio-cultural milieu to another. In most situations, these relationships are based on mutual suspicion and disregard. While Catholics are accused of worshipping images and idolizing Mary, the indigenous African Churches are accused of syncretism, and the Pentecostals are perceived to be proselytizers and scam artists. At best, their relationship can mostly be described as a mutual tolerance or intolerance. The possible avenue by which these Christian traditions ever come together is usually under the auspices of the association of Christian churches in each particular church or region as the case might be. In Nigeria for instance (and this Nigerian example is almost the exact template of the same situation along the governments and peoples of the coastline of West Africa), Christians come together under the auspices of the Christian Association of Nigeria (CAN). Before CAN, the Nigerian Anglican/Roman Catholic Commission (NARCC) had existed as an ecumenical body wherein joint days of prayers for unity are held, and theological discussions ensued.

Upon the arrival of the Pentecostals, and in light of the unstable economic and political situation in the country, it was imperative under CAN to have a common voice facing the new political realities in the nation. There have been calls to prayers nationwide and several communiques and papers presented commonly from CAN in response to burning social issues at different times. CAN came to birth out of necessity; in 1976, the military government had invited religious leaders to the State House at Dodan Barracks, Lagos to discuss some of the government social policies which were to be introduced into primary and secondary schools. The religious leaders took a cue from the meeting and decided to form CAN out of the existing Christian Council of Nigeria (CCN), which at the time now includes the Catholic Church and two other groups placed under the title "Others": the Aladura Churches comprising mainly of the AICs and the Evangelical Fellowship, which will later morph into the Pentecostal assemblies. CAN is organized on zonal, state, and local government levels with women and youth wings. CAN can also boast of a National Executive Council made up of 105 members responsible for electing a "rotational" presidency, they also have a general assembly consisting of 304 members responsible for ratifying the president's election.[29] The idea of rotational leadership already speaks to disunity in there ecumenical endeavors. This has affected the process of election into office those to be entrusted with leadership. It is not uncommon to find corrupt practices of political negotiations and rumors of bribery and government involvement in CAN's electoral processes.

A PENTECOSTAL PERSPECTIVE ON ECUMENISM

Pentecostals generally seem ambivalent when it comes to the question of ecumenism. Neo-Pentecostals in the West who are beginning to build a viable theological base are willing to engage in ecumenical encounters better than evangelical and neo-Pentecostals found mostly in the Southern Hemisphere. Based on my fieldwork and research findings, Pentecostals in West Africa think that ecumenism is important but, in reality, I did not find many instances of ecumenical associations between Pentecostals, Catholics and other denominations. There are a few instances where Pentecostals had to work with other denominations borne out of an immediate expediency. For instance, in Sierra Leone, immediately after the civil war and the aftermath of the Ebola decimation, a coalition between churches was formed to try and respond to the humanitarian needs at the time.

Various reasons militating against the possibility of ecumenical association are enumerated in chapter 6. This situation is one of the examples that show the state of Christianity in its supposed glorious upsurge on the face of the continent. Interestingly, Frank Macchia provides damning evidence by calling attention to "the tongues of Pentecost." Macchia avers, "The tongues of Pentecost may provide a pregnant metaphor for a distinctly Pentecostal reflection on ecumenical exchange with Roman Catholics."[30] Macchia clarifies further, "The tongues event of Pentecost exposes the scandal of both a complacent sectarianism that offers no need to strive for unity and a complacent Catholicism that is convinced such unity already exists."[31] Because the Pentecostals lay claim to the centrality of "tongues" as it was given on Pentecost day, Pentecostalism cannot be sectarian, therefore must be ecumenical. Macchia goes further stating,

29. Ijezie, Audu, and Agnes, *Church in Nigeria*, 51–52.
30. Macchia, "Tongues of Pentecost," 2.
31. Macchia, "Tongues of Pentecost," 2.

> The event of Pentecost by nature resists domestication as a metaphor that inspires the narratives of just one movement or segment of the people of God. Pentecost is an ecumenical event. It should make Pentecostals feel uneasy and insecure within the closet of Pentecostal piety. It urges them to come out of that closet and to discover 'pentecostalism' in communions other than their own, especially in ways unfamiliar to them. It reminds them that being Pentecostal in the full sense of the word means transcending the boundaries of the Pentecostal movement in directions unexpected and quite dramatic. It means, in part, facing the ecumenical promise and challenge implied in the presence of the Roman Catholic Church.[32]

To focus on the mystery and transcendence of tongue-speech, according to Macchia, is an important theological foundation for understanding and affirming diversity among the various Christian traditions. Language, culture, and doctrinal traditions are relative to the mystery of God who is present in these diversities of traditions where diversity stands for the communion of a free humanity with a free, self-revealing God. Macchia therefore concludes that "such diverse communions can fellowship and work together as equal partners as they dialogue across ecclesiastical lines. Tongues as a *prodigium* that breaks in upon us from God's spirit functions on one level as a kind of 'anti-language' that reveals the utter futility of any effort to attribute status to any one language of faith."[33]

Allan H. Anderson, one of the most acknowledged theologians to have carried out thorough research on Pentecostalism views the connection between ecumenical work and contemporary Pentecostalism as almost void. Anderson posits that despite the belief of evangelicals and Pentecostal dating back to Azusa Street, it was presumed that this new surge of the spirit will become an *apostolic faith*. This idea, that the Pentecostal movement will sweep over the known Christian church, holds sway to date, and more so in the nerve center of neo-Pentecostalism of the Southern Hemisphere. Anderson asserts that Pentecostals saw unity in a spiritual sense, but not a unity in creed or doctrine. Anderson alludes to one area in which ecumenism seems to function, even if not profoundly taken to heart: the interaction between Pentecostals and charismatic renewals in the older Christian traditions. Anderson argues, "At grassroots level, the Charismatic movement brought people together from many different denominations in an

---

32. Macchia, "Tongues of Pentecost."
33. Macchia, "Tongues of Pentecost," 8.

unprecedented way . . . 'A sense of unity was generated through the sharing of the divine experiences in the spirit which washed away denomination barriers at the grassroots level.'"[34] Anderson concludes that the greatest weakness of modern Pentecostals is their inability to embrace their potentials for ecumenical diversities and unity.

A seeming lack of interest on the part of Pentecostals in questions of political engagement, struggle for liberation, and freedom from political oppression and social justice widens the gap and makes ecumenical work more difficult. In West Africa, one gets a sense of disconnect between social involvement and evangelism in the Pentecostalism common to the region. While they fill up auditoriums and stadiums for revivals and crusades, most of them are unable to put programs in place which supports social services.[35] Both Pentecostals and older Christian traditions are guilty of building social services like schools and hospitals which most of their congregants cannot afford monetarily to use. This is very prevalent across the board on the West African coast. It is easily noticeable in private secondary schools, polytechnics, and universities owned by Pentecostal pastors or General Overseers (GOs). This extreme lack of social consciousness builds a wall that wedges any kind of effort at ecumenical embrace. According to Anderson, for the Pentecostals, "There has not been a clearly articulated theological foundation for social ministry."[36] Contrarily, they seem to focus on what Anderson refers to as an "otherworldly" spirituality that avoids "worldly" issues. Most prominent and at the forefront of Pentecostal evangelism is material wealth, suppression of demonic forces, healings and miracles, and speaking in tongues—all of which will not feature on the agenda of an ecumenical meeting.

Thomas Rausch opines that the vast majority of Pentecostals are not interested in ecumenism for various reasons, which includes but does not exhaust the reason that many Pentecostals do not know about ecumenism because many of their pastors do not have any ecumenical experience or

---

34. Anderson, *An Introduction*, 252.

35. While one must not make a blanket statement or overgeneralize on this matter, it must be stated that, in the more established Pentecostal churches, there are those who have some welfare plans for economically disadvantaged members. For instance, in Nigeria and Ghana, there is clear evidence to show that some needy Pentecostal members are provided raw food, and are given financial support to pay hospital bills, school fees, or in some instances, some amount to start a personal small-scale business. The problem occurs when you look at the wider picture.

36. Anderson, *An Introduction*, 278.

theological understanding of what this means and entails. Because they have an ecclesiology of restoration, which already sees a spiritual unity of the churches but leaves no room for visible unity, ecumenism therefore naturally contradicts Pentecostals' ecclesial identity.

CONCLUSION

Fifty years after Vatican II, the post-conciliar church has shown remarkable interest in ecumenism. However, the church continues to face other challenges, new and significantly different from ecumenism. Theologians are taking on more contemporary problems like ethics, climate change, politics, war, and problems arising from the church having to confront a society and culture that is constantly evolving—plural and secular. There seems to be a dichotomy between "parish-Catholicism" and Catholicism which is intellectually and theologically involved. We have, in modern times, progressives and conservatives in traditional Christian communities. The more recent Christian Pentecostal/charismatic churches seem all to be ultra-progressives with no time to devote to theological or doctrinal debates. Ecumenism no longer enjoys the front burner as it did in the sixties, seventies, and early eighties. It will seem from my reading that activists like Yves Conger have slowly faded into the sunset. The idea of ecumenism is reduced today to the possibility of general assemblies devoted to discussing the same issues without so much as making advances in any direction forward or backwards.

The local efforts, especially in developing nations of the Southern Hemisphere are quickly hijacked along national, ethnic, cultural, and linguistic divides.[37] The polarizing conditions in West Africa includes a plethora of problems like ethnicism, poverty, illiteracy, irresponsible and corrupt governments, and the inability of church leaders to distinguish from the

---

37. Jerry Pillay has the following to say which buttresses the point I wish to make, making reference to the state of ecumenism in Africa, "has entered its winter of despair, is in a state of institutional crisis, is disorganized and is struggling for survival . . . ecumenical voices have become silent, weak, or compromised. Added to this was the crisis faced by the World Council of Churches (WCC) and the All Africa Conference of Churches (AACC), which were struggling to survive financially. Whilst the situation may have changed considerably since then—as the WCC and the AACC have now re-structured themselves, set new goals and vision, and worked on financial sustainability—the reality is that ecumenism in Africa is still under pressure theologically, contextually, and institutionally." Pillay, "Ecumenism in Africa," 635.

myriad of churches who can at the very least be considered genuine different from a scam artist. The future of ecumenical work in West Africa is not clear at this time. It is my hope that, some day, in the not too distant future, Christian churches in poor regions will be truly interested in coming together to support the masses who are already confined to the margins and backwoods of civility, and that modern ecumenists will be prophetic in liberation more than the jamborees of prayer camps, night vigils, and crusades—which oftentimes are simply fleecing a lamb that has already lost its wool. While our ecumenical work may not be focused on theological and doctrinal matters, it may pay close attention to social and economic self-help projects. This battles poverty, provides food for the family table, provides a roof over heads, a bed, and a secured economic base for people. I have found this to be true wherein some churches they have engaged in micro-funding for members.

"*Veritatem facientes in Caritate*"—The truth in a Spirit of Charity

If we live by the truth and in love, we shall grow completely into Christ, who is the head by whom the whole body is fitted and joined together, every joint adding its own strength, for each individual part to work according to its function. So the body grows until it has built itself up in love.

—Ephesians 4:15–16

3

Pentecostalism

AT THE TURN OF the twentieth century, Pentecostalism in Sub-Saharan Africa had become a phenomenon that no serious scholar of Christianity or other religions could ignore. Through its evolutionary stages from the 1920s, Pentecostalism (for various reasons which we shall explore later) continued to grow and expound, thereby affecting the societies it exists in on all fronts: culturally, economically, socially, politically, and religiously. Consequently, it is said that "the Pentecostal genre of Christianity is becoming the dominant form of Christianity in contemporary Africa."[1] Cephas Omenyo, reflecting on the genre which in and of itself is not mono but existing in pluriformity, asserts that Pentecostalism "is a label for that genre of Christianity that claims to be distinctive as a result of its stress on the experience of repentance, personal salvation, and a changed life because of the power of the Holy Spirit."[2] Omenyo goes further to state, "The variety and diversity of African Pentecostalism is palpable. It is sometimes suggested that we should speak of 'African Pentecostalisms' rather than 'African Pentecostalism' because of the existing complexities of categorization."[3] The diversities spoken of here deserve another script and research, starting from classical to neo-Pentecostals of contemporary times.

Pentecostalism takes its roots from the early biblical church of the apostles. What the Pentecostal church teaches is foundationally an attempt

---

1. Robeck Jr., and Yong, *Cambridge Companion*, 132.
2. Robeck Jr., and Yong, *Cambridge Companion*, 133.
3. Robeck Jr., and Yong, *Cambridge Companion*, 133.

to replicate the buoyancy of the freedom and spontaneity of worship of the first century church. The New Testament books of the Acts of the Apostles (and in some of the apostolic epistles) speak of the manifestation of the Holy Spirit on Pentecost day, and several instances after. The usual characteristic features of pneumatic charismata include the abilities to speak in tongues, perform miraculous healings, prophecy and exuberance in worship and praying. While Pentecostalism/charismatic movements have taken hold of the Christian church in the world today, it must be clarified that all Christian churches are necessarily and ontologically Pentecostal. The birth of the Christian church on Pentecost day, the impossible division of the trinity in the life of a faith community, and the promise of Jesus that the Holy Spirit will remain with the church makes any kind of spurious claims to exclusive ownership of the Holy Spirit redundant and untrue. Neo-Pentecostalism, as we shall see later, is another phase in the growth of the Christian faith and one out of many ways by which people can approach God.

Allan Anderson makes a very important distinction, which is oftentimes overlooked or not kept in perspective at all. Anderson reverts to the practice of charismata in the early church through the patristic age to its decline. Starting with second century Montanism, charismatic in nature, claims that spiritual gifts of the Holy Spirit given to the apostles were restored in their movement. Montanus, the leader of the movement, encouraged speaking in tongues, prophecy, and progressive revelation. Among the early church fathers who exhibited and supported charismata in the Catholic Church: Tertullian, Ignatius of Antioch, Clement of Rome, Justin Martyr, Irenaeus, and others. Though from Origen and the rejection of Montanism, public or popular exhibition of charismatic gifts declined, but the church has never denied the power of the Holy Spirit or the manifestation of its powers in Christians and within the ecclesial communities. Scholasticism seems to have been at odds with public expressions of charismatic gifts; as a matter of fact, the outward expressions of charismata were the same evidence for demonic possession: the ability to speak previously unknown language; the ability to reveal unknown facts or secret events of the past, present or of the future; the ability to display powers beyond such individual's age or natural condition; the power of levitation of self or objects; and so forth. It seems that through the Reformation, the Protestant churches were more weary of spiritual gifts which were argued to have been needed only in the Church of the Apostles. There were however, fringe or sectarian groups like the Anabaptists, who were associated with

Thomas Munster, who were rejected by Luther for their public display of charismatic gifts.[4] According to Anderson, although rejected by mainline Christianity, sporadic outbursts of charismata happened till the nineteenth century. It was only at the emergence of John Wesley's Methodism, German Pietism, and the Holiness Movement in the nineteenth century that there was a resurgence of charismatic phenomenon. By the end of the nineteenth century, the ground work for Pentecostalism was laid in American revivalism with the idea of baptism in the Holy Spirit. Anderson avers,

> The many and various revival movements at the turn of the twentieth century had the effects of creating an air of expectancy and longing for Pentecostal revival in many parts of the world. The signs that this revival had come would be based on the earlier reports: intense desire to pray, emotional confession of sins, manifestations of the coming of the Spirit, successful and accelerated evangelism, and spiritual gifts to confirm that the power of the Spirit had come. And as a result, various Pentecostals revival movements broke out in various parts of the world in the first decade of the twentieth century. Bolstered by earlier revival movements in the nineteenth century, especially in the Holiness and healing movements, this coming of the Spirit was linked to a belief that the last days had come, and that the gospel was to be preached to all the nations of earth before the soon coming of the Lord. The stage was set for the new Pentecost to spread across the world in the (twentieth) century.[5]

Many martyrs, mystics, saints, and ascetics in the history of both Western and Eastern rites of the Catholic Church have a great history of charismatic gifts. In fact, central to the theology of worship in the Eastern rite is pneumatology and the gifts of the Spirit. In the West, from the turn of the nineteenth century, contemplatives, Desert Fathers, hermits, monks, nuns, and laypersons have continued to exhibit privately and publicly charismatic gifts which continue to revitalize the gift of faith and the life of the church. While it is true that the Roman Church for some reason, over time, downplayed public expression of charismata, it remains a gift that the church recognizes it as a manifestation and presence of the Holy Spirit in the church. For instance, for anyone to be declared a saint, there is a need for witnesses to charismata of some sort, which would either have been manifested while the candidate for sainthood was alive or after his or her demise. As the

---

4. Anderson, *An Introduction*, 22–24.
5. Anderson, *An Introduction*, 38–39.

Catholic Charismatic Renewal emerged from the late seventies and early eighties, a renewed attention to pneumatology began and prayer meetings witnessed the manifestations of the Holy Spirit.

It can be successfully argued that Pentecostalism is the fastest growing religious phenomenon around the globe currently. Some call it a revival of traditional Christianity which is said to have grown lukewarm. Cardinal Walter Kasper calls this a "third wave of Christian history," or a third phase where mission is no longer *"ad gentes"*—to the nations/peoples of the world, but *"inter gentes"*—between peoples of religious commitment.[6] This growth is adduced to evangelical movements, Pentecostal churches, and charismatic movements. The relationship between evangelicals, Pentecostals, and charismatics cut across the board and point to the need for an ecumenical dialogue if this neo-pneumatological movement is to truly impact the churches, especially in Africa. To accomplish this, Michael Fuss states that it is only through a self-humbling on the part of each group: "a humble *diakonia* of truth which serves those who seek, and recognize the signs of the times in today's culture through which the divine Spirit speaks, often in surprising ways."[7] The idea that all tension between the new Pentecostals needs resolution for its evangelism to reconstruct the Christian faith and its expressions in the cultural milieus can be found. Fuss says this is the tension between what the message of revelation is *saying* and what the church is *hearing*. Speaking of this tension, Fuss states that confusion among these groups is apparent given the four coordinates of the exhortation to the churches: "Hear what the Spirit says to the Churches."[8] Fuss argues further to clarify "the dialectic between the living 'Spirit of God' and the structured 'churches' *(ekklesia)* in an ecumenical setting. These four points join up across the field of tension between historic event of Pentecost as the official birthday of the Church, and original Pentecostality (or immediacy of the Spirit) of the Christian faith that is still antecedent to the former event, and continues to inspire and update it."[9]

---

6. Müller and Gabriel, *Evangelicals, Pentecostal Churches*, 9–10.

7. Müller and Gabriel, *Evangelicals, Pentecostal Churches*, 11.

8. Müller and Gabriel, *Evangelicals, Pentecostal Churches*, 11.

9. Müller and Gabriel, *Evangelicals, Pentecostal Churches*, 12. Fuss goes on in his work to state, "This process of rethinking, and of adopting dual perspectives on ecclesiality . . . with reference to the polarity of the Church—based and extra-ecclesiastical popular religion, and the need to integrate it . . . Evangelicals, Pentecostals and Charismatics are children of their times, and their new forms of ecclesiality have emerged in direct response to societal problems. Social changes resulting from globalization, new

Pentecostalism and Catholic Ecumenism In Developing Nations

Pentecostalism accounts for a very considerable number of followership currently in the growth of Christianity in Africa. It is also currently the fastest growing face of Christianity in South America, and in some parts of Asia. While no one is certain about numbers, a conservative estimate situates its numerical strength at around 600 million adherents.[10] These numbers are conservative estimates, but it is sure that the numbers are still on an upsurge curve. It indicates a phenomenon that is constantly being studied in the demographics of world Christianity and world religions. For instance, there are no current statistical data available to cover many West African countries from which the fieldwork and research for this project was conducted. Major cities in West Africa are homes to a wide range of Pentecostal churches, mega-churches, faith communities, and other charismatic faith communities found in traditional missionary oriented churches. Numbers cannot be tabulated accurately because many of the Pentecostals criss-cross carpets from traditional Orthodox churches to the white garment *Aladura* churches and back to Pentecostal assemblies.[11] Walter Hollenweger, one of the leading scholars of the history and growth of the Pentecostal church asserts that looking at the geographical breakdown, it reveals a shift from a predominantly white Christianity to what he calls "the indigenous non-white or to the third world Pentecostal Churches."[12] This phenomenon has been baptized and renamed many times over. For some scholars, the paradigmatic shift of the "new" face of Christianity to the Global South is a new Pentecost. For some others, it is a new Reformation or a third wave in the history of Christianity. According to Thomas Rausch, the first wave

---

patterns of thought and behavior in emerging post-colonial and postmodern cultures, and unforeseen reactions to inculturation processes need to be carefully analyzed with respect to their prophetic dynamics." Müller and Gabriel, *Evangelicals, Pentecostal Churches*, 15.

10. Müller and Gabriel, *Evangelicals, Pentecostal Churches*, 1.

11. Müller and Gabriel, *Evangelicals, Pentecostal Churches*, 1. For further studies in the area of statistics, the late David Barret and Todd Johnson are referenced as experts for consultation. Since the growth of the Pentecostal church is still very much on the increase, all figures are invalidated within two to three months. According to Allan Anderson, "scholars of Pentecostalism both within and without the movement use these figures with abandon to claim that Pentecostalism is the second largest force in world Christianity after Catholicism. They do not always point out that most of the 600 million people are not classical Pentecostals and are predominantly Africans, Latin Americans and Asians. It is on these three continents where the greatest expansion has occurred, despite the obvious and continuing significance of Pentecostalism in North America and in Europe." Müller and Gabriel, *Evangelicals, Pentecostal Churches*, 4.

12. Hollenweger, "After Twenty Years' Research," 403–12.

of Christianity's history is represented by the historic churches of the first millennium. The second wave is referred to as the confessional churches of the Reformation, while the third includes dynamic pneumatic, evangelical, Pentecostal, and charismatic movements of the 1900s.[13]

Walter Hollenweger asserts that a look at the geographical breakdown of the spread of Pentecostalism currently reveals that "the overwhelming part of this Christianity belongs either to the indigenous non-white or to the third world Pentecostal Churches. Taken together with general trends in the Roman Catholic and Protestant churches, this indicates that the numerical and perhaps also the spiritual center of Christianity will shift away from white Western forms to this new type of Christianity."[14] Hollenweger opines that the global expansion of Pentecostalism, disdained initially because of its black roots, despite all odds, still evolved to a global dimension. (Peculiarly the same situation was true in Africa where the indigenous Pentecostal African prophet/preachers were looked down upon.) This worldwide expansion, according to Hollenweger, is not based on organization or doctrine, since both are not consistent with Pentecostalism. Hollenweger ascribes Pentecostal growth to the following;

- Orality of worship;
- Narrativity of theology and witness;
- Maximum participation at the levels of reflection, prayer, and decision-making, and therefore a form of community that is reconciliatory;
- Inclusion of dreams and visions into personal and public forms of worship that function as a kind of icon for the individual and the community;
- An understanding of the body/mind relationship that is informed by experiences of correspondence between body and mind—the most striking application of this insight is the ministry of healing by prayer.[15]

Orality—vibrancy of Pentecostal worship—is a simpler means by which theology and social values are carried on in a very specifically oral society. The individual plugs into the memory of a community which is far simpler to decode than rigorously thought out theological stand points.

13. Rausch, "Catholics and Pentecostals," 930.
14. Hollenweger, "After Twenty Years' Research," 3.
15. Hollenweger, "After Twenty Years' Research," 6.

Hollenweger argues that the consequences for this insight are far reaching. Hollenweger states that the majority of Pentecostal churches develop their own theological positions, liturgy, and organizational structures. According to Hollenweger, "for them the medium of communication is, just as in biblical times, not the definition but the description, not the statement but the story, not the doctrine but the testimony, not the book but the parable, not a systematic theology but a song, not the treatise but the television program, not the articulation of concepts but the celebration of banquets."[16] Pentecostalism sells itself because they present an alternative form of worship which is more spontaneous—perhaps even entertaining—than the somber atmosphere prevalent in traditional Christian liturgies.

Quite a good number of Pentecostal scholars agree that there is no one adequate definition prescribable for Pentecostalism.[17] It is at best descriptive of churches and movements whose emphasis is on a pneumatic understanding of the practice of the Christian faith. Also, Pentecostal identity enjoys a constantly changing face, while its major characteristics remain homogeneous, or at the least, essentially close. The Pentecostal movements are classified under classical Pentecostalism, charismatic Pentecostals, and neo-Pentecostals. Classical Pentecostals usually are classified with traditions rooted in the African Independent Churches (AICs), like the Assembly of God Church, International Church of the Four Square Gospel, The Church of God in Christ, or those first generation churches who confess

16. Hollenweger, "After Twenty Years' Research," 10.

17. Robeck Jr. and Yong in their seminal work state, "in recent years, significant changes have taken place in the writing of Pentecostal history. Voices from around the world, voices that we have not heard from previously, or have been ignored by earlier Pentecostal historians, are increasingly involved in these discussions. Regional histories are emerging with the result that the findings of earlier, more general histories, originating mainly from the United States, are being challenged and in some cases set aside . . . the growing complexity of the term Pentecostal and its modifiers has led a number of historians to observe that no single definition for the term may any longer be possible. One must now think of Pentecostal movements (plural) with multiple definitions." Robeck Jr. and Yong, *Cambridge Companion*, 1–2.

They pay attention to a fundamental problem with external materials coming from earlier sources outside of Europe and America: "Most early sources and histories till extant were written in English or in some other Western European language. Most American historians of Pentecostalism have not studied any of the available sources outside of the English language . . . When these factors are placed alongside the fact that many early resources from other parts of the world have not been as diligently preserved as European and American resources have, it becomes clear that writing a complete and objective account of the early Pentecostal period is extremely difficult, if not impossible." Robeck Jr. and Yong, *Cambridge Companion*, 15.

the baptism in the Holy Spirit, biblical evidence, and speaking in tongues.[18] Charismatic Pentecostals are those who exist within the older Christian traditions, especially from around the 1960s and the birth of the Catholic Charismatic Renewal in 1967.[19] They pay attention to healings, expulsion of demonic forces, laying on of hands, and anointing with oil. The third group referred to as neo-Pentecostals or neo-charismatics include a cross section of evangelical Christians who disassociate themselves from older traditions. They focus on miraculous healings, exorcism, the fight against the devil and his agents, and setting people free from ancestral curses. Some also stress the idea of tithing, selling of blessed articles purported to contain healing powers, or "sowing seeds," which means to give some money in trust for God's return of the worshipper's requests.[20] It is worthy of note that this work pays attention fully to neo-Pentecostals always with a view in one's mind of their direct link to classical Pentecostalism of the AICs. There is the "'charismatic movement," which reflects a renewed pneumatological space akin to Pentecostalism in the Catholic Church.

A BRIEF HISTORICAL BACKGROUND: ORIGINS AND EVOLUTION OF PENTECOSTALISM

The history of the renewal of the Pentecost event in the church as it has evolved into contemporary Pentecostal movements takes two forms. Western and European scholars tend to locate the origin of the renewal to the Azusa Street mission of 1906, borne out of an African American prayer group in Los Angeles.[21] Some other scholars from South America,

18. Ukpong, *Nigerian Pentecostalism*, 61.

19. Rausch, "Catholics and Pentecostals," 930.

20. While I subscribe to this three prong understanding of the classification of Pentecostalism as a religious phenomenon, Thomas Rausch present five types worthy of mentioning: (1) Classical Pentecostalism, (2) Indigenous denominations, (3) Independent neo-Pentecostals, (4) Charismatic renewal, and (5) Proto-charismatic Christians. Rausch affirms that these classifications are not always clear cut. Rausch, "Catholics and Pentecostals," 931.

21. This also is debated by some other scholars who give credence to the missionary work of Charles Parham in Texas where Pentecostal charisms had already been experienced before the Azusa Street prayer meeting. Of the Azusa Street ministry, Thomas Rausch writes, "It was extraordinary in a number of ways. First, those coming to the mission rejoiced in extraordinary gifts of the Holy Spirit, including an ecstatic form of worship. Second, though it originated in an African American prayer meeting in a still segregated Los Angeles, the congregation was soon interracial, with blacks and whites

Pentecostalism and Catholic Ecumenism In Developing Nations

Asia, and Africa trace a different historical origin different from the Azusa mission. For instance, Ogbu Kalu, in his seminal work on Pentecostalism, clarifies that from the very beginning, "African Pentecostalism did not originate from Azusa Street and is not an extension of the American electronic church."[22] For Kalu, African Pentecostalism was as a result of the response to missionary enterprise by the indigenous African Christians (also known and referred to as African Independent Churches, AICs).[23] Citing as an example the Ethiopian movement, which was an attempt at a recovery of African identity through religion, Kalu makes the claim, "Ethiopianism was a muscular movement that operated with a certain theodicy claiming that God has not deserted Africans to their humiliation but has raised a people to restore Africa's lost glory."[24] This, Kalu perceived to be an African spirituality that will be anti-structure and anti-colonialism which will give birth to a vibrant nationalism. It will empower and energize African Pentecostalism post-independence. It should be noted that these AICs are inherently reactionary to both the colonial masters and the newly educated African elites who became urbanized, occupied government positions and quickly disassociated themselves from the uneducated class.

In an attempt to get a clearer picture of African Pentecostalism, for this work and the Pentecostalism that is common to the West African coast, I must agree with Ogbu Kalu's summation. The AICs fall primarily into classical Pentecostalism. Reactionary or not, they appropriated some of the traditional "charisms" of Africa's primal religions without necessarily labelling everyone syncretists. Kalu argues further that all forms of religious expressions rely on the resources of indigenous cultures. For a native people to be able to appropriate any religion, they necessarily fall back on their previous religious experience accounting for the attraction of Pentecostalism itself

---

praying and singing together. Third, from its beginnings the movement spread like wildfire. Within six months, members and others interested in the Azusa Mission had founded several new congregations in Los Angeles and its environs. Its participants held meetings in neighboring communities, often in tents or rented storefronts. By September, its evangelists had traveled from San Diego to Seattle, by December they were active across the country, and at least 13 missionaries had been sent to Africa. In the next two years the movement spread to Mexico, Canada, Europe, Africa, even to Northern Russia." Rausch, "Catholics and Pentecostals," 928.

22. Kalu, *African Pentecostalism*, viii.

23. Other designations for the AICs include African Initiated Churches, African Indigenous Churches, and African Independent Churches.

24. Kalu, *African Pentecostalism*, viii.

Pentecostalism

to the African purview.[25] For Kalu and I add myself to those who belong to this group, only ourselves can tell our own stories. It is important for us to tell these stories properly to situate how this phenomenon has evolved and where it is today, different from where it was when we started. According to Kalu, "It is germane, therefore, to separate the background and early charismatic movements in the colonial period from the developments in them post-independence period, especially those occurring from the 1970s onward. The nature, goals, tools, strategies, and leadership of the battle for identity through religious power changed under new circumstances, but the goal remained the same."[26] There is a clear distinction between the Pentecostal movements through the decades; this makes labelling difficult, but makes contextualizing a necessity. In proper context, therefore, one can historically begin to see the emergence of African Pentecostalism, revivals, and identity from 1900 to 1960. Various indigenous "prophets" were already traversing different parts of Africa from 1910, when European missionaries were gathered in Edinburgh to discuss further mission work in Africa. With the advent of the Second World War, and the strong imperial and colonial hold on Africa, "African response included subversive rumors, nascent political mobilization, and a plethora of radical religious movements predominantly bearing the marks of charismatic spirituality."[27] Kalu sums up this all important clarification as follows,

> From the historical discourse, it can be demonstrated that the movement in Africa did not start from Azusa Street . . . I conclude that a charismatic wind blew through the African continent in the post independent period that first hit the youth and women, and later overawed the resistance of the mainline Churches. In each country, certain socioeconomic and political factors determined

---

25. Kalu expounds on this thinking averring, "the cultural discourse foregrounds the fit of the Pentecostal movement into the indigenous worldviews as an explanation for the attraction and growth of Pentecostalism, imaged as a religious response to the three publics—the indigenous 'village' public, the emergent urban culture, and the intruding Western public. Each public purveys certain values. It is argued that scholars have tended to start from and end the study of African Pentecostalism with contemporary, urban emergent cultures of Africa and have lost sight of the vitality of the movement as it engages the village public (where most Africans live and have their being) and later, in reverse flow, the Western public." Kalu, *African Pentecostalism*, xi.

26. Kalu, *African Pentecostalism*, xi.

27. Kalu, *African Pentecostalism*, xi.

the pattern of the early concerns. But various strands connected across national boundaries.[28]

This argument does not exclude a variety of missionary influences. What remains clear according to Kalu is that the emergence of missionary evangelical Pentecostalism came to Africa to find these religious impulses already in existence. While they initially coexisted, various factors forced a separation. African Pentecostalism took its roots from the indigenous impulses.[29] One cannot argue successfully that it has remained the same ever since. But as many scholars are quick to point out, Pentecostalism has evolved in every decade and continues to do so in contemporary time. According to Birgit Meyer, a huge world of difference exists between the world of the traditional image of an African prophet of the Nazirite, Zionist, or Aladura Pentecostal churches. Dressed in a sashed white gown (soutana), armed simply with a cross, a bell, and the Holy Bible, barefooted, he went from street to street at the crack of dawn to announce the imminent return of the Lord and invited the people to repentance. As a young boy between the age of seven to ten years old, the voice of the prophet woke me up daily as early as 5:00 a.m. He cut a figure of a Nazarene with his scraggly beard, red bloodshot eyes, and dreadlocks, and packed it into his chef-like top hat. This Pentecostal prophet stands in contrast to the flashy neo-Pentecostal pastors of the new multimedia, multi-million dollar, mega-Pentecostal assemblies. Meyers aptly describes them thus,

> the flamboyant leaders of the new mega-churches, who dress in the latest (African) fashion, drive nothing less than a Mercedez Benz, participate in the global Pentecostal jetset, broadcast the

---

28. Kalu, *African Pentecostalism*, xi.

29. Kalu surmises the situation at the time in the following succinct words, "Classical Pentecostals appeared early in the African religious landscape and operated with a muscular indigenous agency to charismatize Africa . . . The crucial point is that none of the classical forms of Pentecostalism became important in the religious landscape until they benefitted from the spiritual renewal of the 1970s . . . and certainly counter the impression that 'new crusaders' recently forayed into Africa bearing the insignia of fundamentalism.

Pentecostalism emerged from the indigenous response of Africans to the missionary message; the missionary input from evangelical ministries such as Scripture Union, Campus Crusade, and such; from the increasing missionary forays of Pentecostals from the holiness tradition and Pentecostal denominations from various countries who utilized the labors of African agents; and from interdenominational parachurches, bolstered by the educational institutions of many American Bible colleges and many evangelical evangelizing outreaches." Kalu, *African Pentecostalism*, 64.

message through flashy TV and radio programs, and preach the prosperity Gospel to their deprived and hitherto-hopeless born again followers at home and the diaspora. Although it would be too simple to assume that the latter simply replaced the former, the emergence of these new figures suggests that the appropriation of Christianity in Africa has entered a new phase.[30]

In the emergence of this new face of Pentecostalism, a typological distinction is made between the AICs, the first wave of neo-Pentecostalism, and the current mega auditorium and jet-flying Pentecostalism. The development and timeline seem to be one and the same along the West African Coast and in Africa, generally.[31] Meyer concludes that, given the current state of African Pentecostalism, its classifications and categories can give way to, "albeit contested, processes of de-essentializing such notions as African, authentic, or local, detemporalizing tradition, deconstructing modernity, blurring the boundary between religion and politics, and even deuniverlizing religion."[32] Whatever the case might be, Pentecostalism, especially of West African persuasion, continues to expound and enlarge. For instance, J.D.Y. Peel notes, "The Yoruba have exported their brand of neo-Pentecostalism all over sub-Saharan Africa, especially to major cities like Nairobi and Johannesburg. And in Europe too, whether to serve mainly their own diaspora or to light the Pentecostal fire in a native white population (as with the Embassy of God in Ukraine.)"[33] All over Europe and America, Pentecostals offer a chaplaincy of welcome and safe haven for the throngs of African migrants. From my personal experience, most Africans who arrive in Europe and America, and who practice the older forms of Christianity, usually have problems with "somber and solemn" liturgies they see. Unlike the celebratory and lively worship at home, the migrant encounters a cold and impersonal style. In some instance, their white hosts fail to extend a

---

30. Meyer, "Christianity in Africa," 448.

31. Meyer expounds on the all too common features of the new Pentecostal leadership in the following way: "Many PCCs present themselves as ultimate embodiments of modernity. Building huge Churches to accommodate thousands of believers, making use of elaborate technology to organize mass-scale sermons and appearances on TV and Radio, organizing spectacular crusades throughout the country-often parading foreign speakers—so as to convert nominal Christians, Muslims, and supporters of traditional religions, creating possibilities for high-quality Gospel Music, and instigating trend-setting modes of dress all create an image of successful mastery of the modern world." Meyer, "Christianity in Africa," 459.

32. Meyer, "Christianity in Africa," 467.

33. Peel, *Christianity, Islam*, 214.

hand of welcome and, sure enough, they begin to "shop" around. Once they have found the Pentecostal communities, they immediately feel at home. They network and are helped to settle down, get accommodation, jobs, and social security cards. Even for the illegal immigrant, he finds welcome and fellowship.

Pentecostals in the diaspora fulfill a role the older generational churches are mostly unable to fill. They believe there is a trend which constitutes a "major paradigmatic change in the Christian mission, popularly labelled a 'reverse mission.' African Pentecostals are convinced that God's mandate to them is to reach out to the entire world. This conviction is captured by their including words such as 'global,' 'international,' and 'world' in their nomenclature."[34] And gradually, Pentecostalism is beginning to impact the host European and American communities. Perhaps the Pentecostals will be at the forefront of the re-evangelization of the global West. Cephas Omenyo expresses the situation in the following aptly descriptive terms, "The growth of African Pentecostalism . . . is perceived by Africans as a relevant religion in that it is scratching where the African is itching the most, because it takes the African world view seriously by responding to the issues that emerge from the African scene, a feat that Western theology has not been able to accomplish adequately."[35] Omenyo concludes that this is the foundation for the "Pentecostalization" of Africa, Europe, and America.

PENTECOSTALISM, POLITICS AND SOCIAL IMPACT

It is an accepted reality that Africa remains the fastest growing face of modern Christianity. The Pentecostal phenomenon is a big part of this reality. Naturally, Christianity impacts various countries of Africa from many perspectives and dimensions. From my fieldwork in West Africa, in every one of the four countries I conducted my research, both historically and currently, each country has experienced and continues to experience the Christian church, particularly Pentecostalism, in different ways. The focus of my research is to explore if the new Pentecostal presence has had any part to play in already unstable ecumenical efforts of the pre-existing older Christian traditions, and to see if these new *"Spirit-filled"* movements have any impact on questions of social justice, governance, economy, and politics.

34. Robeck Jr. and Yong, *Cambridge Companion*, 144.
35. Robeck Jr. and Yong, *Cambridge Companion*, 147.

Most researchers who have made significant contributions to the study of Neo Pentecostalism usually do not make concise connections between Pentecostalism, politics, and social impact. It is true that many government officials along the West African coastline are known to frequent prayer camps and pastors. They ask to be prayed over for protection against evil forces and the possible machinations of political opponents who may be arranging a quick meeting with the creator through assassination. They also flock to these "miracle grounds" close to election times. Some politicians become "born-again" Christians with public manifestation of a newfound faith. It has been suggested that such conversions may be true, but they are politically motivated to canvass for votes and seek support of the Pentecostal community, whose numbers are quite formidable in an electoral process. A good example is that of Mathieu Kerekou of Benin, former dictator, Marxist, and commander in "thief," who bankrupted his country during a seventeen year mis-rule (1972–90). According to Paul Gifford, Kerekou had "been the first African dictator to fall in the second liberation struggle, was reelected to power—this time not as a Marxist but as a born-again Christian. In 1996 there was no political mileage in Marxism, but a great deal in Pentecostalism."[36] It is also a plus for pastor/church that catches the *big man* in government. In a sense, it is a win-win situation when this happens. It is not unusual in Nigeria and Ghana to hear stories of Pentecostal pastors' complicity in money laundering, exchange of monetary gifts from politicians for prayers, or huge donations made from government coffers to church projects. Brigit Meyer asserts that Pentecostals are more of a political opportunist, "they walk the corridors of power . . . and align themselves with the government."[37]

In Ivory Coast, there is a story which is not far different from the story of Mathieu Kerekou of Benin. On August 21, 2010, President Laurent Gbagbo of Ivory Coast, along with his supporters and the Pentecostal assemblies, celebrated the fiftieth anniversary of the country at the Felix-Houphouet-Boigny stadium in Abidjan. This celebration expressed the sentiment that it would be a turning point in the history of the nation. It would witness the nation's liberation from demonic forces hampering the development of the nation. With the born-again leader, President Gbagbo, this idea of political and religious liberation was tied to a politically driven agenda of national reconstruction or second founding. This will be marked

36. Gifford, *African Christianity*, 34.
37. Meyer, "Christianity in Africa," 465.

as a break with the immediate past-post-coloniality of Ivory Coast, this was named *refondation*. The Pentecostals also saw this as the rebirth of a nation now baptized in Christ. Ivorian and researcher of religion, Konstanze N'Guessan, appraises this situation and queries why born-again Christians in Abidjan and the Gbagbo government appropriated a national celebration with a premillennial theology to transport its meaning into public political discourse. N'Guessan states, "This is a selective approach that does not take into account the position of secular Ivorians or Muslims, let alone people 'in-between' such as born again Christians who support Quattara (the opposition) or Muslims who support Gbagbo."[38] So, it came about that through the "Pentecostalization of the electoral process in 2010 with both Quattara and Gbagbo claiming victory, a civil war lasting six months broke out and at least 3000 Ivorians perished."[39] N'Guessan notes that having allowed "prophecies" and biblical text into politics, and having created "messiahs" out of politicians, Pentecostal influence did not help the political process in Cote d'Ivoire. Rather, the born-again Gbagbo saw himself as the "chosen one," placed alongside the Refondation. Gbagbo could not step down when the opposition won. N'Guessan concludes, "The vitality and violence of this symbiosis cannot be sufficiently explained by instrumentalist theories or assumptions of hidden agendas fueled by power or greed."[40]

Until very recently in Nigeria, the Pentecostals distanced themselves from social actions. In Ghana, while historically the Pentecostal churches have been largely quiet, from time to time, one or two pastors stand in opposition either to a political party or politician. The history in Ivory Coast is unclear, but looks rather more on the side of silence. In Sierra Leone, a different situation exists which I will review in chapter 5 as part of my

---

38. N'Guessan, "Côte d'Ivoire," 82.

39. N'Guessan, "Côte d'Ivoire," 87. According to N'Guessan, Gbagbo is not the first president to develop a quasi-religious status. Felix Houphouet-Boigny was referred to as savior and as quasi-mythical *nan-gama* (Malinke, literally "come for that purpose"), believed to live up to a foretold destiny. *Apotre de la paix*—"Apostle of peace"—was and continues to be a common epithet for Houphouet, who replicated Saint Peter's Basilica in his hometown of Yamoussoukro . . . one stained glass window shows Houphouet as one of Jesus' disciples.

N'Guessan, "Côte d'Ivoire," 88. Apart from the well-established pattern of savior-president, the model of the chosen nation also has precursors in the colonizers, who called the coast of gold, ivory, palm oil and rubber the "land of Canaan. Many Cote d'Ivoire ethnic groups have myths of origin that include an exodus leading to Cote d'Ivoire and thus turn Cote d'Ivoire into the Promised Land." N'Guessan, "Côte d'Ivoire," 88.

40. N'Guessan, "Côte d'Ivoire," 94.

fieldwork report. It is sufficient for now to state that the experiences of a civil war and the decimation of lives by Ebola, followed by a mudslide, gave the Pentecostal and older traditional churches an incentive to come together and act decisively on the side of the people. The situation in Sierra Leone thus becomes a unique case along the West African coast. Major Pentecostal assemblies rely on "faith gospel" which extols the right of born-again Christians to blessings of good health, material success, and protection from evil forces, won by Christ through his redeeming death on the cross. According to Paul Gifford, "Faith Gospel has proved very functional among the religious entrepreneurs who constitute the media evangelists, for its 'seed faith' idea has brought in the enormous resources needed to sustain these extremely expensive ministries"[41] This form of Christianity thrives because it provides a creative response to many destabilizing aftereffects of failing or failed political systems. Gifford clarifies the strength of religion, which is fundamentalist in nature and reactionary, but oftentimes neglects its political and social role, thus,

> A religion provides definitions, principles of judgement and criteria of perception. It offers a reading of the world, of history, of society, of time, of space, of power, of authority, of justice and of ultimate truth. Religion limits or increases the conceptual tools available, restricts or enlarges emotional responses, or channels them, and withdraws certain issues from inquiry. It inculcates a particular way of perceiving, experiencing and responding to reality. Religion can legitimize new aspirations, new forms of organization, new relations and a new social order. Every religion involves struggles to conquer, monopolize or transform the symbolic structures which order reality. All these are issues for political analysis, and issues that are missed if questions of the political role of religion are asked purely in terms of church versus state.[42]

It is clear that Pentecostal churches are focused on liberating people from physical and spiritual bondages. But it seems they prefer to do this from a purely spiritual warfare; this includes the realization of the very profoundly expressed gospel of prosperity. In the Pentecostal churches where business and finance matters are taught, it is not devoid of sowing seeds and paying tithes. According to John Mansford Prior, Pentecostalism has yet to understand "the imperative of channeling its formidable power into the needs of

---

41. Gifford, *African Christianity*, 39.
42. Gifford, *African Christianity*, 26.

the temporal world, towards the gospel call to transforming the social order according to the plan of God."[43] John Prior asserts that Pentecostalism "has confined itself to a spirituality of conversion, of holiness and fellowship, failing to galvanize its adherents into a force of advocacy and action against the structures of sin."[44]

The newest breed of sleek Pentecostal pastors—which I will like to name as *Pentecôtistes nouvelle génération* (PNG)—are known for their mega auditorium-based assemblies. They employ elegantly dressed, manicured, and trimmed pastors as living examples of those whom God's favors rest. These assemblies are oftentimes "churches" for middle to upcoming and upper class, new money and affluence. These are faith communities where businesses network, connect, and thrive. The congregation has a good number of single, successful bachelors and spinsters who meet to date with the hope of ending in marriage. The PNG are a totally new breed of classy Christians, jet set, and extremely generous in "sowing seeds." The new age pastors are a crossbreed between motivational speakers, marriage counselors, life coaches—even boot camp instructors and preachers. The new appeal is focused on a gospel that assures its adherents of material wealth and success. The pastors are adept at fundraising for projects which raises further funds for ministry. Tithes and good will seed sowing are fundamental to receiving God's blessings. As a glaring example: "'Daddy and Mummy in the Lord" (that will be pastor/general overseer and his wife)—their opulence and wealthy lifestyle is an example of being blessed by God. This includes expensive jewelries, apartments/mansions, a fleet of expensive vehicles, and, in some instances, a number of private planes. More worrisome with PNG and contemporary Pentecostal leadership is the often touted and spurious claims of personal visions and messages from God. While the adjudication on whose visions and messages are true or not are difficult to navigate, the rate at which the visions and messages come questions the validity of the self-revelation of God in the sacred texts of the Scriptures.

It is exactly because of this kind of extensive and powerful outreach of popular religion, in the face of the spread of Pentecostalism on the continent, that forces one then to question a seeming lack of interest either in politics or social-justice questions. Gosbert Byamungu notes that despite Pentecostal attraction, it remains a fact that they do not have a serious

---

43. Müller and Gabriel, *Evangelicals, Pentecostal Churches*, 255.
44. Müller and Gabriel, *Evangelicals, Pentecostal Churches*, 255.

social agenda on the growth of the indigenous people: "They tend to be eschatologically oriented, promising salvation in the world to come. Apparently the only people with access to salvation also in this world are the organizers—who in the process net a great deal of money! They tend, also, to depend on and be uncritically guided by models of life and programs 'made in the USA.'"[45] The traditional churches have (and some continue to) played pivotal roles in politics and social issues by issuing pastoral letters, participating in national debates, and acting as watchdogs on issues of governance, elections, social justice issues, and corruption. Pentecostalism, with its numbers, is naturally expected to collaborate in ecumenical efforts, particularly when it speaks to social justice issues. As it will be further clarified in chapter 5, under fieldwork report; on paper, West African Pentecostals (pastors and adherents) agree that ecumenism that pays attention to social justice issues is essential. However, in reality, this is not true.

THE FUTURE OF PENTECOSTALISM IN WEST AFRICA

Pentecostalism in West Africa has its own face, context, and some unique flavors. While Pentecostalism has grown following the trend we have earlier set (classical, charismatic, neo-Pentecostals), there is yet a most recent and yet to be named trend of Pentecostalism (those I refer to as *Pentecôtistes nouvelle génération: PNG*). This newer form of Pentecostalism is easily noticeable through social media and by my encounter through fieldwork. Neo-Pentecostal pastors who have roots going back to classical Pentecostalism agree with me that this new phase in the development of this phenomenon raises more questions than give answers. In some ways, it lays the groundwork for beginning to imagine what the future of Pentecostalism may look like. It also forces the question of what possible ecumenical encounter may be made possible for the future. This newest phase and face of Pentecostalism has not shown any interest in social action of any sort. The future of Pentecostalism, in its varied forms as found along the West African coast, is almost impossible to predict because of its amorphous and ever-shifting features.

This question cannot be answered succinctly because the failure or upward progress depends on God's will and volition. And in some ways, on how successful and progressive Africa's nascent democracies grow. If countries continue to wallow in abject poverty and the private usurpation of

---

45. Byamungu, "Constructing Newer 'Windows,'" 346.

public resources by the elitist/political class, most Pentecostal communities will continue to grow. One of the social functions Pentecostalism provides is a social cushion from the fall out of many of African's failed or failing nation states. The Pentecostal movement provides hope against the misery and suffering of the people at the hands of unjust and unscrupulous politicians and their foreign allies. They also give a sense of protection from the dark forces which proscribes the "success and destiny" of many in Africa. They promise health and wealth in the face of all pervading anthropological poverty of a people. However, if Africa turns a new leaf, and we have credible governments and thriving economies, then as it has always been in history, the need for God and his immanence becomes secondary at best. When the people can pay for state of the art medical treatment, receive the best possible quality of education at all levels for their children, have access to public infrastructure, and assured security, religion, especially in its more flamboyant style, is most likely going to be relegated to the background. People tend to become more "sophisticated," and will seek out the expression of Orthodox religion which is oftentimes associated with the elites and intellectually aware of society.

There are chances that those who were proselytized into neo-Pentecostalism may have reason(s) to return to their original faith base. The tension between older missionary styled Christian traditions like Catholics, Anglicans, Methodists, and so on, accounts for a high percentage of Pentecostal adherents and followers.[46] Reasons for this large shift, especially among the young and middle age, are often adduced to a cold and impersonal European style of worship and a stifled opportunity to encounter the Spirit of the living Jesus in worship and prayers. However, the animosity caused by the proselytizing of the Scripture Unions (known as SUs) in the tertiary institutions across West Africa in the 1980s and 1990s remains a divide yet to be bridged. As it is true of many Pentecostal churches, the SUs cajoled and lured other Christian students into their prayer meetings with the promise that it is a non-denominational gathering of Christian brethren. They then set to work by slowly indoctrinating them with the use of "biblical texts" carefully pre-selected which will contradict the doctrinal understanding of their would-be convert. Most of the mega-Pentecostal assemblies in Nigeria, Ghana, and Sierra Leone started out in this same way. Cephas Omenyo explicates on this situation as follows,

---

46. Rausch, "Catholics and Pentecostals," 935.

In Nigeria, the Universities of Ibadan and Ife were the major centers of the Charismatic revival in the early 1970s. However, by the mid-1970s the Charismatic revival in Nigeria had gained strength and spread beyond the university campuses into the wider society, and most Charismatics in that country are still educated elites who are generally fluent in English ... By the 1980s the movement had assumed a high social profile owing partly not only to the attention given to it by the media but also to multitudes of new churches and "ministries" that were emerging and erecting signboards all over the major cities in Africa ... and most of the evangelistic programs and healing and miracle services of this group of ministries are targeted at urban dwellers, particularly upwardly mobile youth.[47]

One of the earliest things that made Pentecostalism appeal to a wide range of people is its experiential African world view of mystical and diabolical causalities. The African mind is always alive and aware of these realities. By proclaiming a revival that is at the least interventionists and intercessory, this promotes an adequate sense of security and hope for the African. As I have mentioned earlier on, Omenyo agrees with my position stating, "Pentecostals have developed religious rituals that serve as a survival strategy to economically and socially disadvantaged Africans ... An African style of worship and liturgy and a holistic Christianity that offers tangible help in this world as well as in the next together constitute a uniquely African contextualization of Christianity."[48] In most prayer tents, revivals, auditoriums, or gathering spaces of Pentecostal all across the board, the eternal warfare between the Holy Spirit and the world of darkness rages on for the souls of humanity. Exorcisms and the casting out of offending spirits are common, making pastors with the powers of healing very sought after. Again, Omenyo asserts, "Divine healing is at the core of Pentecostal and charismatic ministries. Pentecostals offer 'Christian' variations of indigenous etiologies of illness, and these are overcome by their practice of divine healing."[49] Considering the mindset of Africans and the belief in a world of witches, wizards, and negative spirits, coupled with lack of adequate medical infrastructures in most places, to be sucked into "Spiritism" is quite easy and understandable.

Wolfgang Vondey suspects that the malleability and subsequent growth of the Pentecostal movement includes also what he chronicles thus:

47. Robeck Jr. and Yong, *Cambridge Companion*, 137–38.
48. Robeck Jr. and Yong, *Cambridge Companion*, 139.
49. Robeck Jr. and Yong, *Cambridge Companion*, 139.

Pentecostalism and Catholic Ecumenism In Developing Nations

> Pentecostalism is an ecumenical melting point. Unlike the many existing churches and denominations that originated in deliberate response to splits and separations resulting from doctrinal and practical differences, Pentecostal communities worldwide did not organize or institutionalize in conscious reaction to particular ecclesiastical patterns. Instead, global Pentecostalism has emerged in both continuity and discontinuity with various existing doctrines, practices, rituals, disciplines, spiritualties, and organizational forms, and the resulting character of Pentecostal groups does not readily form a homogeneous ecumenical picture.[50]

For now, this phenomenal rise of Pentecostalism, especially in West Africa, the locus of my fieldwork, is beginning to experience some rude awakenings. Through the use of social media, the preaching, actions, and money-raising events are coming under public scrutiny and reaction. Online videos abound where Pentecostal pastors (especially the PNGs), do the most absurd things like asking people to eat grass as manna-food from heaven, or stomping on a woman's stomach to cure her of fibroids. One character from Ghana, during one of his prayer services claimed to have had God on hold on his cell phone. There are recurrent reports of miscreant sexual contacts between some pastors who, in the name of praying over people, anoint naked women, fondle breasts, and participate in the touching of female genitalia. In another case, a pastor needed to be carried around the tent of revival because he claimed his feet must not touch the ground while in ministration. In an extra ordinarily bizarre case, a well-known and highly respected Nigerian Pentecostal pastor asked for voluntary donations starting from one billion naira for a church project. It went viral and received negative ratings for insensitivity to the plight of citizens overburdened by government corruption and ineptitude. This request is made of people who make averagely about eighteen dollars monthly to sustain themselves and their families. These are just a few outside of the many extremely outlandish requests of some Pentecostal pastors, all in the name of God.

Ogbu Kalu, a renowned scholar and researcher into Pentecostalism in Africa expounds on the personality cult of Pentecostal preachers thus,

> There is a linkage between the iconic image of the leader, the message, and the lure to mimesis. The dress and lifestyle of the big man of God become essential ingredients of the composite culture . . . Where Paul calls himself a bondservant, the new pastor/shepherd engages in a personality cult, and flaunts his person,

---

50. Robeck Jr. and Yong, *Cambridge Companion*, 272.

> wealth and status . . . the attack on prosperity theology from a certain sector of the same movement used a spiritual index to warn against the 'spirit of things', a materialism that could entrap, capture, and lockup the preacher in bondage in spite of Paul's warning: Love not the world . . . in the media industry, style is important for enhancing the message and the messenger: The glossy photographs of the leader, his wife or family, and members who celebrated happy events serve as mission statements asserting the believer's capacity to refuse defeat from the harsh, disabling environment, and to pose as an overcomer.[51]

Notwithstanding some excessiveness on the part of opportunists who have hijacked the Pentecostal movement for personal gain, one must also acknowledge that there are a few Pentecostal pastors who are truly zealous for evangelical work. In my encounter with Pentecostal bishops, senior and junior pastors, general overseers or founding fathers, I learnt to listen to their convictions and their beliefs. While I am in no position to judge anyone, I can honestly sense that many are into this as a business and money-making venture. Twice, I spoke with a bishop and founder, his honesty and a desire to serve his people convinced me that he was a man truly desirous of proclaiming the good news of and about Jesus Christ. He was the only bishop and founder of a Pentecostal assembly who would sit down and speak with me in four countries and thousands of miles of travel. His vision for his assembly, and his projects which includes care for the poor, showed a side of a Pentecostal pastor that is not commonly seen. On my second visit, I found about thirty people in the waiting area waiting to see him. Since I had an appointment, I was ushered into the bishop's office by an associate. I was made to understand the bishop had left instructions that I should be brought in on my arrival. As we exchanged pleasantries, I casually asked him who all the people out in the waiting lounge were? The bishop explained to me that these were people that his ministry financially supports, those who need help with different situations, and that he is committed to seeing that no one is unattended to. He is the only Pentecostal pastor who is involved in ecumenical work in the countries in which my fieldwork was conducted. I verified his claim that he had worked with the other churches after an aftermath of a national disaster and found his words true. It is also with this bishop that all my questionnaires were returned on time and complete. I attended one service where the bishop was a guest preacher, even

---

51. Kalu, *African Pentecostalism*, 112.

though I could argue one or two theological points, it was yet clear that he is an honest servant of the gospel.

For the Christian message to endure on the continent, the Pentecostals cannot afford to make the same mistakes their older brothers of the older tradition have made in the past: the idea that it is cozy and safe within their own assemblies, thereby becoming exclusive and not desirous of interacting with other Christian churches. The Christian church in Sub-Sahara Africa faces a silent but portent threat from globalization and extreme liberalism. As cultures collide and penetrate each other through technology and the new wave of the internet and electronic media, a common front and ecumenical handshake across the divide is a necessity for the Pentecostals and other Christians. The older Christian traditions can be said to be faring better in terms of moderating the effects of liberalism. However, the Pentecostals are profoundly more impacted since they are mostly offshoot and patterned after American televangelism and mega-churches. When Pentecostalism comes of age, it will have to deal with some moral questions which it does not have to deal with currently. As Africans, the position of African Pentecostals on issues such as feminism versus patriarchy, same sex marriage, transgenderism, abortion, the use of contraception, divorce and remarrying in the church, etc. will most likely take on a different response from their American sponsors. The existing polarities between the Catholic and Protestant churches on these issues are strong indications that the indigenized church in Africa is still in its toddling years. To face the accelerated pace at which our world is evolving, paying attention to heaven, or even social actions are not enough to combat the onslaught of postmodern reality of excessive liberalism which attacks Christian morality.

A second very portent issue, especially in the West African region, that makes ecumenical work a must is the unrelenting insurgency of extreme and radical Islam. Even though this is a global problem, its West African antecedents are unparalleled in Africa. Ibrahim Yahaya Ibrahim in his work notes,

> The recent rise of jihadist movements in West Africa, including Boko Haram in the Lake Chad region and Al-Qaeda in the Islamic Maghreb and its affiliates in the Sahel-Saharan region, has puzzled many observers. The easy spread of the jihadist ideology, the jihadist movements' success in massively recruiting followers among local populations as well as their ability to conquer and administer territories, are unprecedented in the region's contemporary history . . . the phenomenon of jihadist insurgencies in West Africa

emerges as a result of a series of processes at the global, local, and individual level . . . For a wide range of reasons, certain regions of Africa have experienced weakened state capacity and increased local conflict, and it is in these areas that jihadist insurgencies have emerged. At the individual level, the process by which African individuals decide to enroll in jihadist groups include ideological, situational, and strategic motivations, and these have all been facilitated by deteriorating conditions of life in marginalized areas.[52]

In this case, the fundamental question raised about the public role of the Pentecostal assemblies on issues of social justice just got expounded and stretched much further than before. In Nigeria, the hot bed of Boko Haram insurgency, Ghana, and Sierra Leone, skirmishes have been recorded between radical Islamic Jihadists against Christians and sometimes against moderate Muslims who do not agree with them. In Nigeria for instance, there are public statements, unrefuted by the federal government that there is an agenda to Islamize the entire country. In this volatile situation, presenting a common front in protecting the Christian population is a necessity. Also, to be able to prepare and provide for internally displaced peoples (IDPs) is a task that the church must be wholeheartedly committed to.

There is also, on the West African map, a salient but real problem of syncretism or recourse to "the native ways." Many of our poor people are disillusioned to the point that they are skipping around looking for any and all means by which they can access miracles of protection, cures, and overcoming poverty. The gospel of prosperity continually creates hordes of people who will have nothing to do with a suffering servant of Yahweh, the idea of the crown of thorns or his cross. Invariably, after running around many campgrounds, and the miracle they seek not happening, they fall back into one of Africa's traditional religions. The late Professor Bolaji Idowu and a good number of scholars of African traditional religions introduce a more theologated perspective to the question of post-missionary and post-independent Christianity in Africa. Idowu summarizes the situation very succinctly thus,

> What I shall describe with the broad title of 'Ethiopianism' has come into expression throughout Africa to emphasize that the continent is moving actively and purposively to recover her 'enslaved soul'. 'Ethiopianism' has taken various forms, ranging from attempts at the indigenization of the Christian Church, the

---

52. Ibrahim, "Wave of Jihadist Insurgency," 3.

founding of churches by charismatic, Christian African leaders, and the establishment of splinters from the European-dominated churches as separatist churches which are completely free from any form of foreign interference. The significant aspect of 'Ethiopianism' for our purpose is the coming into being of 'churches' which are positive repudiations of Christianity, even though they use the scaffolding of the Christian church to erect new structures for the expression of the traditional religion. There is *Orunmilaism* which adopts the oracle divinity according to the Yoruba as the prophet of God to 'the black race', has found a church in his name and worships Olodumare through him. The emphasis here is the replacement of the 'God/prophet' element of Islamic faith with a 'God/prophet' element of the traditional faith, even though the behavior of the church is patterned after Christianity. We have the *Arousa* of Benin City which was founded by the Oba of Benin with the avowed purpose of helping the Edo people to worship God in the language which God understood! To that end, Osanobwa is worshiped through his son Olokun. The emphasis here is a replacement of the 'Father/Son' element of African Traditional Religion. Again, there is the political church which began as the National Church of Nigeria and the Cameroon, changed its name to the National Church of Nigeria with the separation of Cameroon from Nigeria, and has since moved between a politico-philosophical kind of Africanism and a kind of theosophy called 'Goddianism'. The main emphasis here is a total condemnation of the adoption of any 'foreign' or 'imported' religion by Africans: Africa must recover her soul; she must give the first and supreme position to her own God-given heritage, and be obedient to the teachings of her own God appointed prophets. With 'Goddianism' in mind, it is now permissible, however, to appropriate the best element of the African culture and beliefs; but always, African Traditional Religion must be the religion of every African.[53]

A lack of theological understanding between the older Christian traditions born of the missions and contemporary attraction of Pentecostalism can point only in the direction of more problems for the African church. It seems the future of Christianity lies on the soils and sons and daughters of Africa, yet the issues which disunite us are more than the issues that unite us. Ecumenical work, especially in constant dialogue, is the only way forward if the new Pentecost breathing in the panting heart of Africa will

---

53. Idowu, *African Traditional Religion*, 201–7.

reverberate and will engage in the re-evangelization of lands previously home of Christianity, out of which the good news came to us.

If Pentecostalism in Africa will survive, there is an urgent need for a theological and ecclesiological redefinition of its teachings and "doctrines." There is a need to review its hierarchical/governmental structures. It also must redefine itself and make itself seen as interested in the plight of the marginalized. They must give the poor an opportunity and access to their hospitals and universities. The missiological theology and understanding of "suffering" in Christianity needs reevaluation and rearticulating. To turn completely away from a "suffering Messiah," the Lamb of God, and preach only a gospel of wealth is not only unkind, it is sinful and an unjust structure of sin too—considering more so that the majority of the hordes of people you are preaching to are the suffering and poor masses, already impoverished by every factor that should alleviate their suffering and social status. In this case, Pentecostalism is extremely successful with making religion opium for the people. For Pentecostalism to remain relevant in the next phase of Africa's development on the continent's new nations, its politics will have to be re-defined.

CONCLUSION

Contemporary Pentecostalism has challenged the older Christian churches to become more conscious in their worship in the pneumatological space. If it is perceived either in an evangelical or charismatic way, the Christian church has benefitted from the challenge of Pentecostalism, and the manifestations of charismata are apparent in most charismatic churches today. The *"Pentecostalization"* of West Africa extends beyond Christian churches; it has extended to other faith communities. For instance, in the southwestern part of Nigeria, among the Yorubas, mostly, the Muslims (An-Sarul-Deen/ Ansar-Islam) are now known to hold crusades, revivals, and also night vigils. They have Sunday morning Quranic catechetical schools craftily situated around Christian churches. They often have loud speakers mounted which you can hear clearly half a mile away. Not to mention that this affects churches at Sunday worship. The impact of Pentecostalism is felt in an all-encompassing way. Interestingly, this impact is also felt in the lingo-cultures of ethnic groups. Using Nigeria and Ghana as case study, religious language associated particularly with Pentecostal religiosity has found its way into public subculture. In Nigeria, various expressions have crept into common usage among all; it is common now to hear people say, "it is well," to denote a kind of self-abandonment into the hands of God, in the face of perplexing questions of life. Other similar polemical expressions include, "I rebuke it in Jesus' name," "I decree and declare," and "I prophecy into your life." The founding father of Pentecostal assemblies are usually called "daddy," "my father in the Lord," or, simply, "the man of God." The man of God's wife is usually "mummy" or "my mummy in the Lord." The congregation, especially in Nigeria, Ghana, and Sierra Leone, prefaces their names with "sister" or "brother" to denote familial relationship in the body of Christ. Hopefully, soon, someone will pick up on Pentecostal religious language from common usage to preaching and speaking in tongues as a research component.

As it can be found in any other religion, there are abuses and lapses in some cases which calls to question the validity of some of these "jamborees," and if they qualify to be a Christian gathering or an ecclesial community. And because the Pentecostal communities are new and not so coordinated structurally, it becomes difficult to arrest a growing phenomenon of charlatans hiding under Pentecostalism to defraud, sexually molest, and grow rich on the sweat of already impoverished people. When I asked John Cardinal Onaiyekan, the cardinal archbishop of Abuja, Nigeria, his views, particularly on the proliferation and multiplicity of Pentecostal churches in Nigeria, he answered, "We as human beings are not in position to judge anyone, but history judges us all."[54]

---

54. Oral interview conducted at the archbishop's house, Garki, Abuja, Nigeria, on January 14, 2017. Currently, John Cardinal Onaiyekan is one of the three international moderators of the World Council of Religious Leaders: Religions for Peace (RfP), which has its headquarters at the UN Plaza in New York. He is also the chair of the African Council for Religious Leaders and a cardinal member of the Congregation for the Doctrine of Faith and the Congregation for Divine Worship and the Discipline of the Sacraments, two of the foremost departments of Vatican bureaucracy. Pope John Paul II nominated him as a member of the Methodist-Roman Catholic International Dialogue Commission for a period of ten years. He was president for the Christian Association of Nigeria (CAN), among many other national, regional, and international theological and dialogue appointments.

Whether they will it or not, they are our brethren. They will cease to be our brethren only when they seize to say; 'Our Father.'

St. Augustine, Bishop of Hippo (354–430 AD)

4

Catholic Ecumenism

ROMAN CATHOLIC ATTITUDE TO the question of ecumenism took a positive turn at the convocation of the Second Vatican Council by Pope John XXIII. By naming it an ecumenical council, John XXIII encouraged the council fathers to work assiduously towards the realization of a threefold unity which Christ fervently prayed for among people: unity among Catholics, unity with separated Christians, and unity with others who follow non-Christian religions. It was in the conciliar work of the fathers that the Catholic Church referred to other Christians as "separated brothers" and not "Protestants." And in Catholic relationship with people who practice other religious faiths outside of Christianity, with particular mention of Judaism, Islam, Hinduism and Buddhism, the council fathers stated that the Catholic Church does not reject anything that is true and holy in these religions.

> The Catholic Church rejects nothing of what is true and holy in these religions. It has a high regard for the manner of life and conduct, the precepts and doctrines which, although differing in many ways from its own teaching, nevertheless often reflect a ray of that truth which enlightens all men and women. Yet it proclaims and is in unity bound to proclaim without fail, Christ who is the way, the truth and the life (Jn. 1:6). In him, in whom God reconciled all things to himself (see 2 Cor. 5:18–19), people find the fullness of their religious life.[1]

---

1. Flannery, *Vatican Council II*, 571.

Catholic Ecumenism

With this new self-understanding and approach, John XXIII and the council fathers entered a new phase of Catholic history in its relationship with other churches and ecclesial communities with openness to dialogue and a hope for visible unity. At the conclusion of the Second Vatican Council, the Catholic Church entered into a new era of dialogues and bilateral agreements first between Catholics, Orthodox, and Reformation churches on some key questions like justification, Eucharist, mission and Christology. Later on, a multilateral dialogue ensued between Catholics, Anglicans, faith and order movements, evangelical churches, and the Pentecostal assemblies.

According to Jeffrey Gros, from 1969, the post-Vatican II Catholic Church was fully engaged in ecumenical work at all levels. Gros argues that, first, an internal reorganization laid the groundwork for this renewal. Second, "the recognition of the ecclesial reality of other Christian communities, the acceptance of religious liberty, the recapturing of a unitive understanding of God's revelation, enhanced collegiality and the role of the laity as well as the biblical and liturgical renewal."[2] This commitment was re-affirmed by subsequent popes: from Paul VI, John Paul II, Benedict XVI, and currently, Pope Francis. The creation of the pontifical secretariat for promoting Christian unity remains useful in the pursuance of Roman Catholic ecumenical objectives. A theological principle underpins the Catholic position on ecumenism: the understanding of a real but imperfect communion which joins the Catholic Church to all who profess the name of Jesus as Lord, as well as those who share the same Scripture and common baptism. All of which is expected to lead to three theological Catholic commitments in the ecumenical work: "spiritual renewal, theological dialogue towards full restoration of full communion, and common mission and witness in the world."[3]

In the pursuance of *Unam Sanctam*, the Catholic Church, conscious of itself, insists that, "now as always, as the Church in which the one Church of Christ subsists, and in its own understanding of its own nature (as part of its faith in the whole of the revelation of God in Christ Jesus), it cannot simply concede the same character to the other Churches."[4] The Catholic Church does not see other ecclesial bodies as heretical or schismatic worthy only to be anathematized. "It now regards them primarily as partners in

---

2. Gros, "Toward Full Communion," 26.
3. Komonchak, Collins, and Lane, *New Dictionary*, 317.
4. Rahner, Ernst, and Smyth, *Sacramentum Mundi*, 200.

dialogue and collaboration between Christians who have more in common than separates them and possess a common task in regard to the 'world.'"[5] Notwithstanding this self-understanding, the Catholic Church remains open to fraternal sharing which does not exclude the will to receive and learn from the other: from another's wealth of Christian life, of theology, of charismatic gifts which may not be necessarily present with the same intensity and clarity in the Catholic Church. The Catholic Church seeks an ecumenical union which is clearly understood not to be a return to one church. If true ecumenism is achieved, there will be a new church of the future, details of which will be worked in agreement on liturgy, doctrine, theology, the Bible, etc. In the true spirit of the post-synodal attitude to unity of Christians, the Catholic Church is committed to doing "everything possible which from the point of view of dogmatic and moral theology is *communication in sacris* should not only be tolerated but encouraged cautiously and tactfully, but without undogmatic 'irenism.'"[6] In article 26ff of the Decree on the Eastern Catholic Churches, Vatican II's summary is the succinct description for the *Raison d'etre* for undertaking this work;

> There is a wide field of collaboration available in the duty of all Christians to shape the secular world in a more humane and therefore more Christian way in the social, cultural, economic, political and welfare spheres. In very many respect the Churches acting in common could be the conscience of secular society. In common they could intervene, even in their own ranks, in favor of peace, the abolition of racial discrimination, social justice, the eradication of nationalist prejudices, protection of the poor and weak. For all these purposes common institutions could be set up by common action.[7]

Catholic ecumenism, like ecumenical work, generally, is no longer on the front burner in contemporary times. However, it remains as a central hope of the church. There are more and more issues, newer problems that need evaluation and articulation. However, central to Catholic ecumenical ecclesiology is a "Trinitarian, Christocentric spirituality in which the focus is on Jesus Christ and the action of the Holy Spirit, and which is open to God's direction of the pilgrim people in History."[8] The Catholic Church

5. Rahner, Ernst, and Smyth, *Sacramentum Mundi*, 200.
6. Rahner, Ernst, and Smyth, *Sacramentum Mundi*, 201.
7. Rahner, Ernst, and Smyth, *Sacramentum Mundi*, 201.
8. Rahner, Ernst, and Smyth, *Sacramentum Mundi*, 332.

recognizes that in the mystery of the risen Christ, the "Roman Catholic experience at this moment in history leaves Catholic Christians open to enhancing their own identity by ecumenical dialogue and by the evolution that will be necessary within the Catholic Church to remain faithful to its call to be the sacrament of Christ in the world for the sake of the human community."[9]

A BRIEF HISTORICAL BACKGROUND: PRE-VATICAN II

When Pope John XXIII made known his desire on January 25, 1959 to hold an ecumenical council, he appointed Cardinal Augustin Bea to head the newly created secretariat for Christian unity. Cardinal Bea, originally a Scripture scholar, will emerge to be a leading architect of what later became known as Catholic ecumenism. Archbishop O'Hara, the apostolic delegate to Great Britain at the time, said of Cardinal Bea and his work at the secretariat, "Here are the reflections of a mature mind on the most agonizing Christian problem of our time. They challenge in their own right because of their remarkable combination of patient wisdom with youthful freshness and ardent charity. They are supremely valuable as being the expression of the mind in closest contact with Pope John XXIII."[10] Working with Pope John XXIII, Cardinal Bea presented a new approach, a new emphasis by which the church's language is inclusive and not divisive: "separated brethren" replaced "Protestants."[11] Cardinal Bea was convinced that the work of uniting the church is God's work, and can only be accomplished by God's grace. Therefore, no matter how difficult it may seem from a human perspective, the future remains in the hands of God.

In Bea's reflection within the ecumenical meetings, to grow the appropriate ecumenical spirit, all at the table must acknowledge "truth cannot change but human perception of it can grow in depth and width. No

---

9. Rahner, Ernst, and Smyth, *Sacramentum Mundi*, 332.

10. Bea, *The Unity of Christians*, xii.

11. O'Hara explains further, the new approach that Vatican II will present to the Christian church, "Pope John has given us a lead. In the cause of the unity for which Our Lord prayed to his heavenly father . . . Pope John's own example is an open book which all can read, but in which we, his own children, are intended to read the lesson of a new approach. Formal relations of mutual respect are not enough: they must ripen into friendship. Courtesy must be more than correct; it must be genuinely cordial. Along with the improvement of personal relations must go a better understanding of the mind of non-Catholic Christians: a dialogue, not monologue, at the deepest level."

dogmatic definition can be changed but no dogmatic definition exhausts the truth. The truth revealed by Christ has an undiminished power to teach men lessons which we have not yet learned and accents in which we have not yet spoken."[12] The first point of Christian unity in Cardinal Bea's theological reflection stems from baptism. Even though all are children of God, but the baptized are all a part of the mystical body of Christ which is received only through baptism. Cardinal Bea collaborating with Pope John XXIII created in the Roman Catholic Church an enduring legacy of welcome, open-mindedness, and a fraternal attitude to other Christian bodies. The pope and the cardinal envisioned a future where hostility will be forgotten, all pray and work together to resolve the issues that separates the Christian Church. They proposed three-prong Catholic understanding of ecumenism: first, that an essential notion of unity exists in the Catholic Church according to the mind of the Lord—a unity that is based organically on doctrine, sacraments, and the hierarchical order, made up of the successor of Peter, the successor of the apostles, and clerical family who support them. Second, there is the work of uniting the "separated brethren" with the apostolic see. Third and lastly, this unity cannot be forged by force or cohesion. It is a work of patient, prayerful discernment, and the intervention of the Holy Spirit, so hearts may speak to hearts and differences overcome humbly and with filial affection.

They teach that Catholics must understand that like their separated brethren, we are all born into a tradition. We accept wholeheartedly the legacy (no matter how tainted) handed down by our predecessors. And all of us are convinced that our faith is superior to the others'. They teach that, for any kind of unity to exist, there is the need for humility on all sides, an acknowledgement of mistakes made in the past, and a solemn desire to truthfully come to the table desirous to forgive each other. The octave of prayers for Christian unity, instituted for January 18–25 annually, is placed most significantly between the feast of the chair of St. Peter and the conversion of St. Paul. This event is still held around the world by mainline Christian churches. It is regarded as a first step of unity which then ought to lead into action. Notably, it was recommended that the unity of the churches ought to have a social impact, such as the defense of human rights, the fight to defend religious liberty, the defense of human life from conception to natural death, speaking out against wars, preservation of world peace, and the ecological concerns for our world, among other issues.

12. Bea, *The Unity of Christians*, xiv.

The foundations laid by John XXIII and the work of Cardinal Bea led to a new approach by the Catholic Church post-Vatican II. Many men and women over time will participate in this great work. Their work exists in many commissions' submissions, position papers, and ecclesiastical documents. Bea was strongly involved in the passage of the document *Nostra aetate*, which regulates the Catholic Church's relations with the Jewish faith and other religions. There were young theologians acting as consultants through the council, referred to as *periti*. These men will later on become "giants" in theology and ecumenism. Names like Yves Congar, Henri De Lubac, Joseph Ratzinger, and Edward Schillebeeckx stand out in the academic work of Roman Catholic ecumenism post-Vatican II.

POST-VATICAN II

Pope John XXIII did not live to see the outcome of the Second Vatican Council, which he initiated as an ecumenical council. But the subsequent popes picked up on his wish for Christian unity. Vatican II provides the foundational text by which the Catholic Church engages other Christians in the work of unity. For instance, the decree on ecumenism, *Unitatis Redintegratio*, published November 21, 1964 states,

> Every renewal of the Church is essentially grounded in an increase of fidelity to her own calling. Undoubtedly this is the basis of the movement toward unity . . . There can be no ecumenism worthy of the name without a change of heart. For it is from renewal of the inner life of our minds, from self-denial and an unstinted love that desires of unity take their rise and develop in a mature way. We should therefore pray to the Holy Spirit for the grace to be genuinely self-denying, humble, gentle in the service of others, and to have an attitude of brotherly generosity towards them. St. John has testified: "If we say we have not sinned, we make him a liar, and his word is not in us." So we humbly beg pardon of God and of our separated brethren, just as we forgive them that trespass against us. (UR, # 6–7)[13]

Further on, in article number twelve of the same document, the fathers of the council urge future ecumenists,

> Before the whole world let all Christians confess their faith in God, one and three, in the incarnate Son of God, our redeemer and

---

13. Flannery, *Vatican Council II*, 508.

> Lord. United in their efforts, and with mutual respect, let them bear witness to our common hope which does not play us false. Since cooperation in social matters is so widespread today, all people without exception are called to work together; with much greater reason is this true of all who believe in God, but most of all, it is specially true of all Christians, since they bear the seal of Christ's name . . . It should contribute to a just appreciation of the dignity of the human person, to the promotion of the blessings of peace, the application of Gospel principles to social life, and the advancement of the arts and sciences in a truly Christian spirit. It should use every possible means to relieve the afflictions of our times, such as famine and natural disasters, illiteracy and poverty, lack of housing, and the unequal distribution of wealth. Through such cooperation, all believers in Christ are able to learn easily how they can understand each other better and esteem each other more, and how the road to the unity of Christians may be made smooth.[14]

Since Vatican II, and through the papacy of subsequent popes, significant dialogues have taken place among the Catholic Church of the West and the East. Also between the Roman Catholic Church and some of the churches born out of the Reformation, agreements have been reached on the meaning of baptism, ministry, and certain aspects of the Eucharist. And with Lutheran theologians, agreement was reached on the meaning of justification. Within the progress made so far, issues like the ordination of women presents new obstacles between the Catholic, Anglican, and Episcopalian churches ons. And similar questions like Mariology and common celebration and reception of holy communion.

Paul VI

Giovanni Cardinal Montini was elected pope after the demise of Pope John XXIII on June 21, 1963. He immediately embraced the ongoing synod of Vatican II. Known now as Pope Paul VI, he re-opened the ecumenical council on September 29, 1963, giving the council fathers four key areas as central focus to guide the work of the council: namely, a better understanding of the Catholic Church, the Catholic Church's internal reforms, advancing the unity of Christians, and dialogue with the world. In 1964, Paul VI created a secretariat later renamed the Pontifical Council for Interreligious

---

14. Flannery, *Vatican Council II*, 511–12.

Dialogue for non-Christians, and a new secretariat later known as Pontifical Council for Dialogue with Non-Believers which was created a year later. In 1993 Pope John Paul II incorporated it in the Pontifical Council for Culture, which he had established in 1982. For Pope Paul VI, dialogue with all of humanity was essential as a means to finding the truth. Dialogue, according to him, is based on full equality of all participants. This equality is rooted in the common search for the truth. Paul VI was particular on welcoming some invited Christians to attend some of the sessions of Vatican II as observers. He reminded the fathers of the council to pay attention to the use of language in the deliberations and in the writing of documents so it is truly welcoming and friendly. For Paul VI, the ultimate goal of the council was a universal call to holiness, a call to the fullness of the Christian life, and to the perfection of charity.

In *Lumen Gentium* (the Dogmatic Constitution on the Church), promulgated by Paul VI on November 21, 1964, he avers that by this holiness a more human manner of living is promoted in this earthly society. While ecumenism was central to Paul VI's agenda for the council, he encouraged the council to examine reforms in the church, in the curia, of canon law, and the question of social justice and peace in the world. Pope Paul VI's vision of unity extended beyond the walls of the Vatican; in 1966 and 1967, he engaged in a series of talks with the Communist Party addressing the issues of Christians behind the iron curtain. He was the first modern pope to travel widely during his pontificate, visiting Jerusalem in 1964. He attended the eucharistic congress in Bombay, India and in Bogota, Colombia. He was in Portugal in 1966 on the fiftieth anniversary of the apparitions at Fatima. Paul VI became the first reigning pope to visit Africa when, in 1969, he paid a pastoral visit to Uganda. In October 1965, he became the first pope to visit the Northern Hemisphere when he visited the United States and addressed the United Nations in New York. In 1970, he was in Manilla in the Philippines on a pastoral visit, where an attempt to assassinate him was voided. He became the first pope in history to travel to five continents, and was known as the pilgrim pope. His energy and perspective, which forced him to go out into the world, was part of his ecumenical vision. He wanted to open up the church from its strictly Roman and European strictures. He created new cardinals from outside of Italy more than any previous pope and created a synod for bishops from around the world. In Paul VI's mind, for the church to work for Christian unity, first, the church itself must be united.[15]

John Paul II

Josef Karol Wojtyla was elected pope on October 16, 1978; he took the name John Paul II, and reigned as the supreme pontiff till his passing on April 2, 2005. He was extraordinary in many ways: the first non-Italian to be elected into the papacy in over 455 years; his papacy lasted thirty-two years, making him the second longest papal reign in history; the cause for his sainthood started a month after his death instead of the traditional five-year waiting period; he mastered and had use of twelve languages; he was the most traveled pope in history, having covered 1,100,000 kilometers (680,000 miles) in visits to 129 countries across the world; and he was indefatigable in work and prayers. JPII will later be referred to as "an apostle of ecumenism" who improved the Catholic Church's relations with Judaism, Islam, the Eastern Orthodox Churches, and the Anglican Communion. JPII, as he was popularly referred to, followed in the footsteps of his predecessor popes by calling on all Christians to follow the universal call to holiness; he called the world to a vision of harmony and the values of unity and solidarity. JPII was present and actively participated at the second Vatican Council; he revived the changes brought about by the council. JPII's vision of unity was "journeying together," which is clearly exemplified in his many travels around the world. Clearly seen in the many instances where he called Muslims, Jews, other Christians, and non-Christian religions together to engage in common prayers and fellowship.

In *Unitatis Redintegratio*, the decree from Vatican II on Roman Catholic ecumenism is regarded by many as the *tour de force*, the *intrumentalis laboris* on which ecumenism is premised in the Catholic Church today. Arguably, JPII's 1995 encyclical letter titled, *Ut Unum Sint*, is perceived by many to be a reinforcement and development on the previous work of the council fathers. This letter solidified JPII's efforts in working towards Christian unity. From the first lines of the encyclical, JPII delves deeply into the heart of what unity entails for the Christian peoples, stating as follows,

> *Ut Unum Sint!* The call for Christian unity made by the Second Vatican Ecumenical Council with such impassioned commitment

---

15. McBrien, *Catholicism*, 665–66.

Catholic Ecumenism

is finding an ever greater echo in the hearts of believers . . . The courageous witness of so many martyrs of our century, including members of Churches and Ecclesial Communities not in full communion with the Catholic Church, gives new vigor to the Council's call and reminds us of our duty to listen to and put into practice its exhortation. These brothers and sisters of ours, united in the selfless offering of their lives for the Kingdom of God, are the most powerful proof that every factor of division can be transcended and overcome in the total gift of self for the sake of the Gospel . . . believers in Christ, united in following in the footsteps of the martyrs, cannot remain divided. If they wish truly and effectively to oppose the world's tendency to reduce to powerlessness the Mystery of Redemption, they must *profess together the same truth about the Cross*. The Cross! An anti-Christian outlook seeks to minimize the Cross, to empty it of its meaning, and to deny that in it man has the source of his new life. It claims that the Cross is unable to provide either vision or hope. Man, it says, is nothing but an earthly being, who must live as if God did not exist. No one is unaware of the challenge which all this poses to believers. They cannot fail to meet this challenge. Indeed, how could they refuse to do everything possible, with God's help, to break down the walls of division and distrust, to overcome obstacles and prejudices which thwart the proclamation of the Gospel of salvation in the Cross of Jesus, the one Redeemer of man, of every individual?[16]

JPII goes on to poignantly declare,

> Nevertheless, besides the doctrinal differences needing to be resolved, Christians cannot underestimate the burden of *longstanding misgivings* inherited from the past, and of mutual *misunderstandings* and *prejudices. Complacency, indifference* and *insufficient knowledge of one another* often make this situation worse. Consequently, the commitment to ecumenism must be based upon the conversion of hearts and upon prayer, which will also lead to the *necessary purification of past memories*. With the grace of the Holy Spirit, the Lord's disciples, inspired by love, by the power of the truth and by a sincere desire for mutual forgiveness and reconciliation, are called to *re-examine together their painful past* and the hurt which that past regrettably continues to provoke even today. All together, they are invited by the ever fresh power of the Gospel to acknowledge with sincere and total objectivity the mistakes made and the contingent factors at work at the origins of

---

16. Pope John Paul II, "Letter Enciclica."

their deplorable divisions. *What is needed is a calm, clear-sighted and truthful vision of things,* a vision enlivened by divine mercy and capable of freeing people's minds and of inspiring in everyone a renewed willingness, precisely with a view to proclaiming the Gospel to the men and women of every people and nation.[17]

According to Massimo Faggioli, writing on JPII's reception and continuity with Vatican II, Faggioli states that in the theological reflections on various aspects of Vatican II, when the conversation focuses on ecumenism, JPII is the marker for Catholic ecumenism. Faggioli referred to JPII as the "last guarantor for Vatican II," "sometimes in a rather nominalistic yet unequivocal intention to receive the legacy of the council . . . in his encyclical *Ut Unum Sint* (1995) and interreligious dialogue beginning with the World Day of Prayer in Assisi (1986) and in his travels, especially in the Middle East."[18] Faggioli argues that JPII was actively progressive in his pontificate, stating, "John Paull II's election in 1978 unleashed a new impulse for the reception of Vatican II by a bishop of Rome who, as bishop of Krakow, had been very active at Vatican II in the commission for the drafting of the pastoral constitution *Gaudium et Spes* and later as the author of a bulky commentary on Vatican II."[19] JPII was not unaware of some of the problems that arose post-Vatican II, especially in the "progressive" interpretations of the council in Europe and America. He was quick to address what he referred to as "moral and doctrinal relativism" of the churches in the West. JPII was a strong voice against Western liberalism that created a culture of death, where birth control and abortion are presented as panaceas for world hunger. JPII wrote and taught consistently on the just redistribution of the world's natural resources, on the marital love and self-giving mirrored after the self-giving life of God, and condemned the objectification of women and sex by modern media.

JPII embraced *rapprochement* with the Jews. According to Eamon, Duffy Wojtyla's papacy was remarkable in many ways including JPII's visit to a Roman synagogue in 1986. JPII was also the first pope to recognize the state of Israel. And in a March 2000 visit to the holy land, he prayed at the Wailing Wall in Jerusalem and apologized for Christian atrocities against the Jews.[20] JPII organized various ecumenical prayer meetings in

17. Pope John Paul II, "Lettera Enciclica."
18. Faggioli, *A Council,* 15.
19. Faggioli, *A Council,* 18.
20. Duffy, *Ten Popes,* 135.

Catholic Ecumenism

Rome, Assisi, and wherever he visited people of other faiths. JPII's vision of ecumenism was broad and all-embracing, a labor of love he embraced in continuity with the spirit of Vatican II. Not without criticism from those who suggest that JPII hijacked the progressivism of Vatican II, yet in the memory of JPII, it is clear from popular acclamation, that John Paul II can truly be referred to with the title, enjoyed by only four previous popes: "The Great."

Benedict XVI

Joseph Ratzinger was a young priest and professor of theology when he attended Vatican II as *peritus*—even in this undersecretary capacity, his contributions to his bishop made significant impact in the eventual writing of some of the documents of Vatican II. According to Richard Schenk, the depth of Ratzinger's commitment to ecumenism can be gauged by its ubiquitous presence in his doctoral thesis. As a young professor at the University of Bonn, Ratzinger accompanied Archbishop J. Frings, the cardinal of Cologne to Vatican II official as *peritus*. "Ratzinger not only supported the ecumenical intentions of the council, but he criticized texts of the Council that, oblivious to the voices of the Reformation, suggested an overly optimistic account of the human situation."[21] Schenk avers that in Ratzinger's most successful published work is the post conciliar book titled, *Einfuhrung in das Christentum*, in which Ratzinger "took as its starting point this same sympathy for many key existential instincts of the Reformation, particularly in the analysis of the perennial and the properly contemporary pressures against faith and of our corresponding need for grace."[22]

Years after Vatican II, Ratzinger would rise to the post of full professor of theology; in 1977, he was appointed archbishop of Munich and freising and cardinal by Pope Paul VI. In 1981, he was appointed prefect of the Congregation for the Doctrine of the Faith (CDF), one of the most important dicasteries of the Roman Curia. This was a post that earned him the esteemed respect and sometimes disdain of his contemporaries, for his strict discipline and adherence to the church's magisterial authority, her traditions and doctrines. When he was elected pontiff after the passing of JPII, he chose the name Benedict XVI and indicated from the beginning of his papacy that Catholic-Jewish relations, Christian ecumenism, interreligious

---

21. Schenk, "The Unsundered Net," 293.
22. Schenk, "The Unsundered Net," 293.

and inter-cultural dialogue would be a central focus for him. Schenk states that from the beginning, Ratzinger's theological work consistently worked a synthesis of Catholic substance and Protestant sensibilities. According to Schenk, "This *sensus* for the existential significance of the early Reformation is also documented in numerous ecumenical essays in the decades since the Council. Increasingly, Ratzinger's work complemented this properly ecumenical focus with discussions of non-Christian religions and largely post-religious cultural forces."[23] Ratzinger's theology in Schenk's reading was "dialectic," always identifying and forming key theological questions as new issues arose. Schenk avers, "Ratzinger's theology was from the beginning markedly 'aporetic' one that identified problems and took them seriously."[24] Ratzinger calls for the different confessions to work for unity through their plurality and diversity, a unity which does not decrease self-identity.

In the work of Massimo Faggioli, he notes that, at the fortieth anniversary of Vatican II, a significant event occurred: the death of JPII, the last bishop participant at the council, then the conclave and election that produced Benedict XVI "constituted undoubtedly two important elements in the broad theological and ecclesiastical landscape of the debate on Vatican II."[25] The change in pontificate expounded the debate on the historiographical, theological reception and the legacy of the Council. Faggioli avers that from the beginning of the pontificate of Benedict XVI, "his teachings increasingly renewed both ecclesiastical and public scrutiny on the council, bound up with the question about the legacy of the 'Vatican II era' in the vitality of the contemporary Catholic Church and its impact on the Western world."[26] These teachings refired the debate about the role of the council in the church itself, other than a biased ideological and modernist interpretation of the intentions of the Council thereby sparking a renewed interest in the hermeneutics of Vatican II. This position, according to Faggioli, reopened the debate, "sometimes providing support for the criticisms against the historicizing of Vatican II. It even contributed increasingly to his being read as the pope of the *revanche* against the council—in spite of his having been a theologian of Vatican II."[27]

---

23. Schenk, "The Unsundered Net," 294.
24. Schenk, "The Unsundered Net," 294.
25. Faggioli, *A Council*, 26.
26. Faggioli, *A Council*, 26.
27. Faggioli, *A Council*, 29.

Whatever is said of Benedict XVI and ecumenism, his papacy marked renewed conversations between the Catholic, Anglican, and Lutheran dialogue. He maintained cordiality with Islam, Buddhism, Hinduism, and encouraged dialogues and encounter between indigenous peoples and religions. History will remember that Benedict XVI created the ordinariate, *Anglicanorum Coetibus*,[28] which made it possible for Anglicans to enter the Catholic Church.

Pope Francis

Born in Buenos Aires, Argentina, on December 17, 1936, Jorge Mario Bergoglio is the 266th and current pope and sovereign of Vatican City State. After the resignation of Pope Benedict XVI on February 28, 2013, a papal conclave elected Bergoglio as his successor on March 13. He chose Francis as his papal name in honor of Saint Francis of Assisi. Francis is the first Jesuit pope and first from the Americas; he is also the first from the Southern Hemisphere. He is the first pope from outside Europe since the eighth century. In his pontificate, Pope Francis has been noted for emphasis on God's mercy, his humility, and his concern for the poor. He has made himself an icon of religious peace and he is committed to interfaith dialogue. Because of his South American background, people were curious about his attitude to ecumenism. It was not too long before he showed he was interested in ecumenism, and that he was both willing to follow in the footsteps of his predecessor popes, and more. Pope Francis is credited with creating the new expression "ecumenism of blood," by which he meant all persecuted Christians around the world, especially those who suffer violence and martyrdom.

Francis' pontificate has made profound ecumenical gestures with an attitude of "let us come together and talk." He has shown willingness to go to "others"; in 2014 he met with the Orthodox Churches in Jerusalem; he prayed with Pentecostals, with the Lutherans at the church in Rome, and he was in Lund, Sweden to commemorate the Reformation with the Lutherans, among many other significant gestures of a pope who goes out to

---

28. A personal ordinariate, or more informally an "Anglican ordinariate," is a canonical structure within the Catholic Church established by Benedict XVI's apostolic constitution, *Anglicanorum coetibus* of November 4, 2009, ordinariates were established in order to enable "groups of Anglicans" to join the Catholic Church while preserving elements of their liturgical and spiritual patrimony. They are juridically equivalent to a diocese.

embrace others. Unique to Francis' experience is his first-hand interactions with Pentecostals, evangelicals, and charismatics from his days back in Buenos Aires. Like everywhere else, the Pentecostal/evangelical Christianity is impacting Christianity/Catholicism in Latin America, which historically remains a bastion of Catholicism. While the Holy Father is working closely with other religious bodies present in Rome, it clear that Pope Francis is interested in the global perspective. In his international travels, the pope has made it a point of view to engage other Christians and people of other faiths. Martin Bräuer states that Pope Francis' "visit to the evangelical and Pentecostal *Chiesa Evangelica della Riconciliazione* in Caserta should also be seen in this perspective. Those present for his visit included not only Italian members of the community, but also Evangelical and Pentecostal representatives from Argentina, the US, France, Spain, Canada, and India."[29] In the same Caserta meeting with Pentecostals and evangelicals, Pope Francis agreed that uniformity is impossible at this time, but urged all present to walk together in a "reconciled diversity," where it is possible to work, walk, pray, and seek unity in the truth together.[30]

In the apostolic letter, *Evangelium Gaudium* (EG) of Pope Francis, published November 28, 2013, three sections are devoted to ecumenism per se. However, Francis will return several times in other sections to the idea of *communio* as a Christian united witness in the world. In EG numbers 234-7, Pope Francis proposes a model of unity in diversity, (totally different from the previous models which place the Catholic Church at the center of unity). Pope Francis reflecting on the many confessions, assemblies and churches asserts,

> The whole is greater than the part, but it is also greater than the sum of its parts. There is no need, then, to be overly obsessed with limited and particular questions. We constantly have to broaden our horizons and see the greater good which will benefit us all.

---

29. Bräuer, "Pope Francis," 8. Bräuer states further, "Notwithstanding competition between Catholics and Pentecostals, especially in Latin America, attempts at a dialogue have been made between the two confessional families for quite some time. The Pontifical Council for Promoting Christian Unity has been holding talks since 1972 with 'some classical Pentecostal churches and leaders.' In the fifth phase of dialogue, a comprehensive study text was drawn up: 'On becoming a Christian: Insights from Scripture and the Patristic writings.' Its conclusion calls on Catholics and Pentecostals to examine their consciences 'about the way they have sometimes described one another in the past, for example calling the other a "non-Christian" or a member of a "sect."'" Bräuer, "Pope Francis," 8-9.

30. Pope Francis, *Pope Francis*, 227-28.

> But this has to be done without evasion or uprooting. We need to sink our roots deeper into the fertile soil and history of our native place, which is a gift of God. We can work on a small scale, in our own neighborhood, but with a larger perspective. Nor do people who wholeheartedly enter into the life of a community need to lose their individualism or hide their identity; instead, they receive new impulses to personal growth. The global need not stifle, nor the particular prove barren. Here our model is not the sphere, which is no greater than its parts, where every point is equidistant from the center, and there are no differences between them. Instead, it is the polyhedron, which reflects the convergence of all its parts, each of which preserves its distinctiveness. Pastoral and political activity alike seeks to gather in this polyhedron the best of each. There is a place for the poor and their culture, their aspirations and their potential. Even people who can be considered dubious on account of their errors have something to offer which must not be overlooked. It is the convergence of peoples who, within the universal order, maintain their own individuality; it is the sum total of persons within a society which pursues the common good, which truly has a place for everyone.[31]

In the same document, Pope Francis directly addressing the question of ecumenical work among the churches insists,

> Commitment to ecumenism responds to the prayer of the Lord Jesus that "they may all be one" (Jn.17:21). The credibility of the Christian message would be much greater if Christians could overcome their divisions and the Church could realize "the fullness of catholicity proper to her in those of her children who, though joined to her by baptism, are yet separated from full communion with her"... In this perspective, ecumenism can be seen as a contribution to the unity of the human family... Given the seriousness of the counter-witness of division among Christians, particularly in Asia and Africa, the search for paths to unity becomes all the more urgent. Missionaries on those continents often mention the criticisms, complaints and ridicule to which the scandal of divided Christians gives rise. If we concentrate on the convictions we share, and if we keep in mind the principle of the hierarchy of truths, we will be able to progress decidedly towards common expressions of proclamation, service and witness. The immense numbers of people who have not received the Gospel of Jesus Christ cannot leave us indifferent. Consequently,

---

31. Pope Francis, "Apostolic Exhortation," 234–35.

commitment to a unity which helps them to accept Jesus Christ can no longer be a matter of mere diplomacy or forced compliance, but rather an indispensable path to evangelization.[32]

Pope Francis' style is colored by his experiences in Argentina from where he understood that the Catholic Church must change its attitude from self-reverence and focus on Christ "who came to serve and not to be served." Martin Bauer sums it up, "Francis intends a reform of his own church, so that it becomes primarily oriented to the gospel. Ecumenically, this is a significant option."[33] It is clear that Pope Francis has brought a new trajectory to previous papal ecumenical and ecclesial understanding of ecumenism. Francis speaks from his heart, with the belief that Christians must learn to speak united for human solidarity, justice, peace, and the environment as a needed response to the varied challenges of modern men and women.

Unlike Francis' predecessors, Paul VI, JPII, and Benedict XVI, Pope Francis was not at the council—he was ordained in 1969. But Francis has consistently shown an opening to the reception and implementation of Vatican II. According to Massimo Faggioli, "A core theme of Francis is that the poor and their role in the Church and the society . . . he proposes a radical and continuous need for the Church and Christians to be next to the poor, in the sense of existential and economic poverty."[34] Francis' ecumenism relies foundationally on Christ, the gospel, social justice and a new ecclesiology which welcomes all who call themselves Christians.

CONCLUSION

Vatican II represents a major turning point in establishing the foundations of Catholic ecumenical *rapprochement* and interreligious dialogues on different levels—Catholic East and West, Catholic and Protestants, Catholic and Judaism, Catholic and Islam, Catholic and other faiths, Catholic and Pentecostals, evangelical and charismatic assemblies. Papal tradition post-Vatican II shows clearly that the different popes have shown remarkable openness to Christian unity and the work that needs be done. There are subtle changes from one pope to the other, but each pope, living within their own existential and historical contexts, strives to do the best they can,

---

32. Pope Francis, "Apostolic Exhortation," 224–26.
33. Bräuer, "Pope Francis," 12.
34. Faggioli, *A Council*, 29–30.

so that ecumenical meetings do not become mere words that do not reflect and impact reality. It is clear that on the global stage and in the West, the Catholic Church and Pentecostals have an existing working ecumenical relationship. This is not so true in the Southern Hemisphere. It is certainly not true in almost all cases along the West African coast. This is part of the challenge that the Christian church faces in West Africa and in the developing nations of the world. It is strange in a certain sense that the numbers continue to swell, yet the various ecclesial communities and church remain, at best, estranged brothers who do not speak with each other.

EUCHARISTIC PRAYER FOR MASSES OF RECONCILIATION

For it is truly right and just that we should give you thanks and praise, O God, almighty Father, for all you do in this world, through our Lord Jesus Christ.

For though the human race is divided by dissension and discord, we know that by testing us you change our hearts to prepare them for reconciliation.

Even more, by your Spirit you move human hearts that enemies may speak to each other again, adversaries join hands and people seek to meet together.

By the working of your power it comes about, O Lord that hatred is overcome by love, revenge gives way to forgiveness, and discord is changed to mutual respect.

Therefore, as we give you ceaseless thanks with the choirs of heaven, we cry out to your majesty on earth, and without end we acclaim . . .

From the Roman Missal.

5

Pentecostalism and Ecumenism in West Africa

The Foundational Theological Problems

PENTECOSTALISM'S INFLUENCE AND GROWTH continues to rise daily and shows no signs of waning anytime soon all along the West African zone, and many other places in the world. This is blessing for the Christian church and the good news of and about Jesus Christ. The name of Jesus resounds on the continent and more people turn towards salvation in Jesus Christ. There is a new birth and fervor that this movement calls the church and the world to a renewal in the power of the Holy Spirit which vivifies the believers. On the other hand, Christianity is under siege and a new phase of persecution of Christians has been unleashed in the last decade throughout different parts of the world. A 2016 report by Public Religion Research Institute (PRRI), based in Washington, DC, states

> Christians are the most widely targeted religious community, suffering terrible persecution globally . . . The International Society for Human Rights, a secular NGO based in Frankfurt, estimated in 2009 that Christians were the victims of 80 percent of all acts of religious discrimination in the world, while separate human rights observances corroborate this finding. A report of the US State Department shows that Christians face persecution in over sixty countries."[1]

1. Jones and Cox, "America's Changing Religious Identity."

Pentecostalism and Catholic Ecumenism In Developing Nations

Perhaps these Pentecostal assemblies with traditional Christian churches lifting up their voices in prayers can become strength and courage for the persecuted Christians elsewhere. Perhaps, there is a lesson: the world is to learn by this upsurge in charismatic-Pentecostal Christianity. Whatever the case might be, all will be revealed in time.

There, however, remains some foundational theological inquiries that may be debatable, but are essential issues that need clarification. These questions, as it will be seen, are serious questions that go to the root of what Pentecostalism can be classified as outside of popular piety and acceptance. These questions need to be asked and debated. It is not asked to discredit the Pentecostal form of Christianity; after all, "if they are not against us, they are for us" (Mark 38-40). Professing that Jesus is Lord is enough as a guarantee that we are brethren and sharers in the great commission to evangelize and bring the good news of Christ to all. Consideration must be given for the following fundamental questions. Only when they are dutifully and truthfully examined, can there be a bridge between older traditions and the new Christian movements. What model that bridge will adopt is yet to be seen.[2]

---

2. There have been various models suggested over time in the course of searching for a workable model of Christian unity. The following is a synthesized and abridged version of Robeck's analysis: "Most ecumenists do not question the reality of spiritual unity; they believe that Jesus called for a tangible form of unity so that the world may believe. Through the centuries they have suggested various models for consideration. In 1559 ... the Elizabethan settlement included the Act of Uniformity. It required *conformity to a uniform set of standards* for all English clergy. During the 20th century many independent and free churches advocated what was called *federal Unity*, by which they remained independent but developed covenantal agreements with one another ... within the Anglican world, contended for some form of *Organic Unity*, in which existing denominations would cease to exist, though in their coming together, they would form a new organism with varying practices. Others pushed it further, by arguing that whereas denominations might be *united*, they need *not* be *absorbed* ... Cardinal Willbrands, then president of the secretariat for promoting Christian Unity, suggested a model in 1970 that included the pope overseeing what he described as *communion of communions*. All Christians will come under papal leadership with a common dogma, sacraments, and ministry but with differences in things like biblical interpretation, canon law, liturgy, and spirituality. Within the WCC, the Nairobi Assembly in 1975 set forth a model of *conciliar fellowship*. .. The Lutheran World Federation suggested *unity in reconciled diversity*, apparently in response to the Anglican suggestion of organic unity ... In the end, none of these visions of unity has found universal support. Since the 1990s many ecumenists have moved away from the quest for models ... Primary responsibility for our unity rests with God, but all Christians are called to participate in that call. The second prevalent recognition is that whichever form of unity the church ultimately recognizes, it must reflect the full and genuine *koinonia* that God has already given us. As a result, the search

Pentecostalism and Ecumenism in West Africa

The first and most important query is the theological understanding of what constitutes a church, her ecclesiology, which includes her apostolicity even as it reflects in the creed of the Christian church. The question is posed more systematically by Anthony Akinwale, who locates a disconnection between apostolicity of the church and much-mouthed (much spoken about) rhetoric of pneumatology by neo-Pentecostals. Akinwale makes the case thus,

> It is my contention that the crux of the matter, as far as the challenge of Pentecostalism is concerned, is its lack of memory, which makes it impossible to unite the past and the present in the present. It is in this lack of memory that the point of disconnection with adequate pneumatology is located. An adequate pneumatology recognizes in a valid episcopate a ministry with the charism of discernment. For while there must be no stifling of the spirit in the Church, the Church must also test whether what is being taken as the action of the Spirit can be said to be in conformity with the faith that comes from the apostles. Fidelity to the Church's apostolic origins presupposes that there is memory of apostolic teaching. Whether it is classical Pentecostalism or neo-Pentecostalism, the discontinuity with apostolic origins of Christianity is such that it is impossible to speak of Pentecostalism as a new face of Christianity.[3]

Akinwale argues that the more than two-thousand years of history provides the Christian church a vast space of memory, and those who wish to enter into the church must learn from its memory so as to bring into the existential now defining moments of her rich history. The defining moments, according to Akinwale, is found in the incarnation of Christ, his ministry, and culminating in his paschal event and resurrection, which the church returns to as it is transmitted by the apostles when gathered around the Eucharist. Akinwale's understanding of what church is is clarified in his work thus, "incorporation in Christ through baptism even though necessary condition for Christian communion, is insufficient for full communion with Christ. The integral profession of the faith that comes to us from the apostles through their successors, and communion at the table of the Eucharist are further requirements."[4] Akinwale avers, "A valid

for visible unity will continue, and Pentecostals have an opportunity to contribute to this discussion." Anderson et al., *Studying Global Pentecostalism*, 291.

3. Akinwale and Kenny, *Tradition and Compromises*, 111–12.

4. Akinwale and Kenny, *Tradition and Compromises*, 113.

episcopate and the eucharistic mystery are what Christ gave to the Church so that she should guard her memory and her bearing in her pilgrimage from Pentecost to Parousia."[5] Lacking therefore in a valid episcopate and authentic eucharistic communion, and disconnected from the apostolic faith of the church, Akinwale asserts, "Pentecostalism loses touch with the two defining moments in the history of Christianity. No one can be authentically Christian in the present who has not been faithful to the past of Christianity."[6] Akinwale notes that the memorial we keep by communion enables the church to speak and work for social justice and not to seek "my prosperity" or "my miracle."

Akinwale summarizes his position and concludes thus,

> Pentecostalism is not merely inadequate, it is adulterated. It represents the futile attempt of misguided or unguided enthusiasm because it is an attempt to elaborate a Christianity without memory... I have argued, absence of *memoria fidei* and *memoria passionis* accounts for the stunning silence of Pentecostalism over socio-political analysis in Nigeria. What Nigeria has been hearing from Pentecostal preachers are 'prophetic predictions' that can only reinforce the illusion of development without good governance, and the illusion of eradication of poverty without an intelligent ordering of common life for the sake of common good.[7]

In term of Pentecostalism and the ecumenical work, Akinwale asserts that Pentecostalism is an obstacle. Akinwale states,

> I have no hesitation in asserting that Pentecostalism is a monstrous misconception and dangerous distortion of the gospel. Here one is not merely dealing with an inadequate Christian spirituality but with a big hurdle on the path of ecumenism, an almost insurmountable impediment on the way to a common comprehension of apostolic teaching. The authentic Pentecostal Church described in Acts 2 was characterized by a common comprehension of apostolic teaching. Pentecostalism is an antithesis to that communion precisely for treating apostolic tradition with levity.[8]

Whether one agrees with Akinwale or not, from a purely theological perspective, one cannot deny that there is a problem, especially with

---

5. Akinwale and Kenny, *Tradition and Compromises*, 114.
6. Akinwale and Kenny, *Tradition and Compromises*, 115.
7. Akinwale and Kenny, *Tradition and Compromises*, 122.
8. Akinwale and Kenny, *Tradition and Compromises*, 122–23.

Pentecostalism's lack of connection to the Christian church's rich history and roots in apostolic tradition. The case in my own opinion and research finding is not only that Pentecostalism is an obstacle to ecumenical work, but that Pentecostalism does not approach other Christian bodies as "churches." Most Pentecostals preach and believe that any kind of gathering with other churches is playing with the unredeemed and a "backsliding" in the faith. There is a morbid fear that they may be subsumed into the existing churches. And commonsensically, the issue of authority, leadership, and the control of funds makes the idea of any kind of unity repugnant to GOs and founding pastors.

Second is the spirituality that expounds on a doctrine popularly called the "gospel of prosperity." In a more theologically minded way, it is also known as "Christianity without the cross." Emeka Nwosuh, reflecting on his work in Pentecostal spirituality, sees an auxiliary spirituality which flows from the universal spirituality of the church. The various forms of auxiliary spiritualties are expressed in different forms and modes. Nwosu states that Pentecostal spirituality is nuanced as exuberant and geared towards ecstatic spontaneity, which does not pay attention to any structured liturgy. Individual manifestation of charisms, the fight against demonic forces, and a life of testimony for miracles wrought and received is at the heart of Pentecostals' spirituality. Nwosuh opines that this spirituality appeals more to the psychological dimensions of people with greater preponderance for the emotions. Nwosu also notes, "The verbalization and exteriorization of Pentecostal spirituality is in keeping with its enthusiastic or exuberant character . . . And so, besides the absence of rituals and symbols in Pentecostal spirituality, there is a considerable absence of interiority in its spirituality."[9]

Nwosuh points to Pentecostal "theology," not only of the person's wellbeing, but also of an assured material wealth and success. This sort of preaching, teaching, and doctrine, according to Nwosuh, "has underhandedly created a subtle drive towards materialism. The human hubris for material acquisition is driven by what has come to be designated as the 'gospel of prosperity.'"[10] Nwosuh avers further, "Implicit in this kind of 'gospel' is a subtle denial of the reality of suffering, pain and failure in the Christian mystery. Consequently, there is the fostering of a certain form of

---

9. Akinwale and Kenny, *Tradition and Compromises*, 113.
10. Akinwale and Kenny, *Tradition and Compromises*, 105.

spirituality that does not sufficiently appropriate into the Christian lived experience the deep implications of the mystery of the cross."[11]

I find very educative the short essay penned by Antonio Spadaro, a Jesuit priest and editor of *L'Osservatore Romano*, and Marcelo Figueroa, a Protestant editor for the Argentina version of the same newspaper. They approach the "gospel of prosperity" from a hermeneutic of critical and theological analysis, naming it a religious anthropocentrism which places the wellbeing of human beings at the center of religion and transforms God into a power at the service of humanity: a supermarket of some sorts, utilitarian, eminently sensationalist, and a pragmatic phenomenon. They argue that this gospel is not unconnected with the "American dream syndrome," which drives a lot of immigrants from their homes to seek the promise of a new life in the land of opportunity. Once this ideal was transformed into a religious reality, opulence and wellbeing became the signs of God's favor and blessings conquered by faith. It has spread around the world, thanks to massive media events fueled by neo-Pentecostals and ministries. In this presentation of the gospel, a theological justification is given to economic neo-liberalism thereby creating a minimalism of the suffering Messiah, the power of his cross and the beauty of the true gospel of Jesus Christ. The writers claim that from the Pentecostal preachers' liberalist exegesis of biblical texts taken with reductionist hermeneutic, they inadvertently reintroduced the Holy Spirit placed at the beck and call of all, Jesus transformed into a debtor by his own words, a God reduced to a cosmic bellhop that must respond to every need and desire of his people.

The co-authors point to a salient yet important aspect where the gospel of prosperity can become disastrous: "claiming" the gift of God is taught based on the faith of the one asking, assured by God's words and the prophetic utterances of the pastor. One's faith, the application of appropriate texts of Scriptures, and confessing it by word produces the desired result. According to Spadaro and Figueroa, oftentimes, if these assertions do not end up as winning narratives, it is then the fault of the one praying for not having enough faith. They sum up the situation thus,

> This is why there can be a lack of empathy and solidarity in these cases from its followers. There can be no compassion for those who are not prosperous, for clearly they have not followed the rules and thus live in failure and are not loved by God . . . One of the characteristics of these movements is the emphasis placed

---

11. Akinwale and Kenny, *Tradition and Compromises*, 105.

on the covenant of God with his people . . . they look to the alliance with the patriarchs. So the text of the alliance with Abraham has a central place, in the sense of guaranteed prosperity . . ."The God of the covenants" . . . Christians are the spiritual children of Abraham; they are also the inheritors of the material rights, the financial blessings and the earthly territorial lands. Rather than a biblical alliance, it sounds like a contract.[12]

Closely connected to this theme, the writers note the prevalent Pentecostal notion of a God sowing seeds, relying on such texts as Galatians 6:7; Mark 10:29–30, etc. The notion is "sowing" and reaping the "harvest." Pentecostalism translates this text to mean how much of financial/material gifts one gives determines how much God in return will bless them. The authors note, "The need for a prosperous life without suffering fits in with a client-centered, made-to-measure religiosity, and the *Kairos* of the God of history gives way to the frenetic *kronos* of the real world."[13] I find, core to the work of these writers, a statement that lies at the heart of this theological misnomer,

> In truth, one of the serious problems that the prosperity gospel brings is its perverse effect on the poor. In fact, it not only exasperates individualism and knocks down the sense of solidarity, but it pushes people to adopt a miracle-centered outlook, because with faith alone—not social or political commitment—can procure prosperity. So the risk is that the poor who are fascinated by this pseudo-Gospel remain dazzled in a socio-political emptiness that can easily allow other forces to shape their world, making them innocuous and defenseless. The prosperity gospel is not a cause of real change, a fundamental aspect of the vision that is innate to the social doctrine of the Church . . . The vision of faith offered by the prosperity gospel is in clear contradiction to the concept of a humanity marked by sin with a need for eschatological salvation, tied to Jesus Christ as savior and not to the success of its own works . . . The prosperity gospel gives voice to another of the great heresies of our time, namely Gnosticism. It affirms that reality can be changed by the powers of the mind.[14]

Against any known Christian tradition, Pentecostalism has removed the cross from the center of Christian theology and re-appropriated the space

12. Spadaro, "Prosperity Gospel," #10.
13. Spadaro, "Prosperity Gospel," #11.
14. Spadaro, "Prosperity Gospel," #14.

for blessings and rewards. Baptism in the Holy Spirit for the Pentecostal is an assurance of divine protection from ill fortune, accidents, or sickness. However, from biblical evidence and the witnessing of the patristics, we know this is not true. St. Ambrose, reflecting on the Christian journey from baptism into the kingdom of God, avers, "Now, water without the proclamation of the cross of the Lord is of no avail for future salvation; but after it has been consecrated by the mystery of the saving cross, it is made ready to serve as a spiritual washing and as a cup of salvation."[15]

The expansion of Pentecostalism "has brought along with it an unprecedented fissure in the already fractured Christian body."[16] Pentecostalism in West Africa can easily be seen, in the description quoted in Nwosuh's work, as "the deregulation, privatization and commercialization of religion . . . the inexorable consequence of a pneumatology that is dissociated from ecclesiology, Christology, soteriology and other branches of Christian theology. It is this kind of dysfunctional pneumatology that is at the root of a number of aberrations found in Pentecostalism today."[17] This situation, therefore, makes any possible ecumenical work impossible from the point of view of Pentecostalism.

Third, Cecil M. Robeck, in his work, appropriates six models on which Pentecostal hesitations rest when it comes to ecumenical work. The six models are used here as a framework for the fundamental and foundational questions which need clarification before paving a way forward towards a Christian unity that focuses on social action. Roebeck argues that the divisions in Christianity are exacerbated by an opposing polarity where calls were made "to preserve the 'truth' in ways that divided Christian 'community' in ways that relativized any notion of 'truth.'"[18] By stereotyping and demonizing each other, differences were highlighted and pejorative terms were introduced to create sides vehemently opposite to each other. And as the Pentecostal and independent Christian groups continue to grow, talk of unity is usually suspect among the new religious movements (NRMs). According to Robeck,

> Calls for unity have been confused with compromise. Calls for agreement have been described as demanding mindless conformity. Calls for greater cooperation have been portrayed as

15. *The Breviary*, 306.
16. *The Breviary*, 107.
17. *The Breviary*, 107.
18. Anderson et al., *Studying Global Pentecostalism*, 286.

devaluing the integrity of local congregations and, in some cases, of individual leaders. And calls for surrender to a common ideal have been spun in ways that make that surrender sound like the quenching of the Holy Spirit. As a result, for too many Pentecostals ecumenism is simply unworthy of consideration, a pointless effort, the beginning of a slippery slope that will inevitably lead to unwarranted concessions. As a result, writing about ecumenism from a Pentecostal perspective is a difficult and at times acrimonious task.[19]

Robeck describes six factors he postulates as the cause for Pentecostals' ecumenical neuralgia:

First, Pentecostal pastors and leaders are usually not savvy when it comes to ecumenism. They "typically had little if any firsthand ecumenical experience with those from traditions that unlike their own—Catholics, the Orthodox, Anglicans and even historic Protestants. This lack of direct encounter weighed on their ability to function as ecumenical peers . . . they would assiduously avoid discussions of visible unity that might prove more contentious."[20] From the West African perspective, while Pentecostal pastors are mostly trained and highly qualified professionals in different fields, they lack, mostly, any reasonable level of theological expertise. For many that I spoke to within and outside the research for this work, they view ecumenism as a ploy to be assumed into the older traditions which they claim is dead in the Spirit. For others, they assume it is some political association for arbitration of claims between feuding Christian groups or pastors, or an opportunity to wrest political power from the hands of the older clerics and an opportunity to liaise with the people in the corridors of political power. Pentecostalism makes ecumenical work difficult or unachievable with this sort of attitude.

Second, "while a personal testimony and a divine call are essential for any kind of successful Pentecostal ministry, they are not always adequate when one engages in ecumenical discussion . . . Such a lack of understanding has led some to condemn the entire ecumenical program"[21] This is evident, but must be understood from a psychological perspective. It is the ground for mutual suspicion where, for instance, a Catholic priest may disdain the pastor for lack of theological training. And the pastor dislikes the

---

19. Anderson et al., *Studying Global Pentecostalism*, 286–87.
20. Anderson et al., *Studying Global Pentecostalism*, 286–87.
21. Anderson et al., *Studying Global Pentecostalism*, 287–88.

Catholic priest for his academic pride, which for the pastor is unnecessary for ministry. In the middle of that is one of the biggest stumbling blocks to overcome: the sin of pride on either sides.

Third, "since the 1940s Pentecostals have found their greatest level of acceptance among evangelicals, and many evangelical denominations have strong sentiments against ecumenism. These sentiments reflect earlier battles within the historic denominations from which many of these Evangelical fled or were driven."[22] This attitude of "us versus them" creates and engenders separation, and the creation of camps where "my friend's enemy is my enemy." The creation of clichés in my research findings is not only within evangelical—Pentecostal—charismatics against older traditions, it exists on a very large scale between African Independent Churches (AICs), neo-Pentecostals, and charismatics. In a sense, the infighting oftentimes is about adherents and the numbers game.

Fourth, Robeck alludes to situations where Pentecostals have suffered at the hands of other Christian communities with specific reference to Pentecostals in Italy under Mussolini, with the alleged complicity of the Catholic Church. These claims were never really substantiated by facts and no arbitration process has ever been put in place. While not a common feature in West African Pentecostalism, there is a subtle "cold war" between Pentecostals and especially Catholics. In this West African instance, the accusation is in the reverse. Catholics accuse Pentecostals of "fishing in someone else's pond"—the proselytization of young Catholics and others of the older tradition. The Catholics claim that the Pentecostals do not engage in mission and evangelizing work but "steal" from already catechized and baptized Christians. In West Africa, this is one of the leading causes for a total breakdown with Catholic/Pentecostal dialogue. However, my research shows that there is a validity to this claim. In my questionnaire, the percentage of ex-Catholics and other Christian churches is extremely high compared to those who claim to be born Pentecostal.

Fifth, In West Africa, bad-mouthing the traditional churches as dead in the Spirit, as idol worshippers of statues, and people who do not read the Bible does not work in favor of any possible unity. It is not uncommon at revivals that Pentecostal pastors will openly attack the Catholic Church and the other older churches. Oftentimes, these accusations are baseless, but are tactics to convince their congregants not to return to their former churches. In my research, I sadly found that some of the priests and pastors in the

---

22. Anderson et al., *Studying Global Pentecostalism*, 288.

older traditions are beginning to react as apologists for their churches by demonizing the Pentecostals in return. One can only wonder how much time and energy are expended disparaging each other instead of preaching authentically the good news of Jesus.

Sixth, Robeck's reading of Pentecostal biblical interpretation, right on target, sees and interprets some sections of the bible in an apocalyptic way in which there is a future world where religion becomes corrupt. They see the older tradition to bear the "mark of the beast—the anti-Christ."[23] In this light they perceive that a move to any kind of unity with the older traditions, albeit the Catholic Church, is an unholy alliance. Therefore, "any move towards greater visible unity within the church, holds negative institutional consequences . . . a dangerous compromise that could ultimately move beyond a shared anti-Christian system. Thus they have condemned ecumenism altogether."[24] How does any right-thinking person fall back into the error of "he uses Beelzebub to fight Beelzebub"?

These issues are the theological and, in some sense, practical problems that both the Pentecostal and older traditions have to grapple with in a sincere spirit of fellowship. It is complicated; by human standards they may actually look unsurmountable. The sheer size and number of "churches" being birthed on daily basis, as can be found along the West African coast, oftentimes than not, are very aloof and desire not to have anything to do with other Christians. However, people of true faith and desirous of doing God's will must always remember, "For man, this may seem impossible, but with God, all things are possible."[25] The problem at hand between the NRMs and older Christian tradition is a carryover from the bitter rivalries of the missionaries who came to Africa. Vestiges of this sad interaction are now an inherited part of our various communities of faith.[26] It is also

---

23. The mark of the beast is found in the vision of John in the Book of Revelation 13:1–18 where it talks about two beasts coming out of the abyss and given power to subjugate people. It has generated a good number of opinions and interpretations including some who claim that either the Catholic Church or the pope is the beast referenced in Revelation with the number 666.

24. Anderson et al., *Studying Global Pentecostalism*, 289.

25. Matt 19:26.

26. Ndiokwere, *African Church*. Ndiokwere's work expatiates broadly on the problems associated with ecumenism and the African church. In one of the sections, Ndiokwere notes, "It is self-deception to claim successes where there are not. And if we are to tell ourselves the bitter truth, we may have to accept the fact that ecumenism in the African Church is not an exciting topic. One does not need to travel a long distance in Nigeria or elsewhere in Africa, or read volumes of books to arrive at a disappointing

partly one of the problems of the post-colonial era where Africans had to deal with "national Christians churches," or as it was the case in Nigeria: to struggle between French and Irish Catholics against British Anglicanism. These divisions widened the gaps between the churches and other Christian assemblies.

CONCLUSION

At the heart of all of the problems facing the countries in Africa (either it is political, ethnic, regional, or religious), foundational to them all is a transformational process of nations birthed out of various colonial experiences. Our politics are foreign and our religions are mostly brought to us from another clime (immediately decimating and demonizing what was original to the African consciousness). Post-colonial era, these nations are in the process of finding their own identity and forging a new people. The result has been less than stellar in many of these countries. The same foundational issue has affected the church. The reaction of the self-identity-seeking indigenous and independent African churches of the fifties and sixties evolved classical Pentecostalism and charismatic impulses of the late sixties, seventies, and early eighties. The neo-Pentecostal movement, from the late eighties till now, is fashioned after the mega-churches of American Pentecostalism and is constantly evolving and reinventing itself, continuing to breed newer and numerous forms of Pentecostalism that have gone beyond any kind of classification.

At the root of the proliferation of both the Christian faith and Pentecostalism lies a problem of dialogue and ecumenical interactions. Given the varied socio-economic problems in the Global South, it is a misnomer that religious fervor continues to expand; Africa is now becoming the new face of modern Christianity, with Pentecostalism holding a formidable front. Yet, the indices for sustainable development in all sectors remain low. The higher percentage of citizens is ranked among the poor while a very small percentage of the political/ruling class is corruptly, filthy rich. Christianity should not exist side by side with the subjugation and oppression of the

---

conclusion that the African Church is ripped with rivalries, unhealthy competitions, marked with mutual distrust and skepticism . . . it is all 'lip service ecumenism.' As interdenominational rivalries and fragmentation of already splintered Churches continue to deepen, the newly founded ones devise clever means of separating from parent bodies while assuming autonomy." Ndiokwere. *African Church*, 317–18.

people. Pentecostalism in West Africa, representing the rest of Africa, has not shown enough good faith in this aspect of a united Christian people, with one voice denouncing and fighting back on behalf of the masses. Michael Fuss reiterates the all-important need for ecumenical friendship among the various Christian churches thus,

> the need for a new mode of dialogue with 'New Religious Movements', especially Pentecostal and charismatic movements. Such a dialogue must encompass four coordinates: It must engage at the grass roots level with the religious experience of individuals and new forms of religious socialization; it must observe closely the religious signals within contemporary mass culture, and postulate a more dynamic relationality between Church and society. This will enable those conducting the dialogue to base their approach on the lessons learned from ecumenical and interreligious dialogue, even though they will need to develop a different method for dialogue with the patchwork religiosity of the aforementioned new world religion.[27]

Without this friendly ecumenical dialogue, Fuss argues that the Pentecostality of the church and the call for a "new Pentecost" have no meaning. For Fuss, "the birth of the Church at Pentecost [becomes] a constitutional gift that unfolds its missionary dynamic in every age . . . The universality or 'ecumenism' of the Spirit of Christ that is manifested at Pentecost is the ground of possibility of both the universal catholicity of the Church *(ad extra)*, and the Church as a communion of the Spirit *(ad intra)*."[28]

---

27. Müller and Gabriel, *Evangelicals, Pentecostal Churches*, 25.
28. Müller and Gabriel, *Evangelicals, Pentecostal Churches*, 32–33.

EUCHARISTIC PRAYER I

To you, therefore, most merciful Father,
we make humble prayer and petition
through Jesus Christ, your son, our Lord:
that you accept and bless these gifts,
these offerings, these holy and unblemished sacrifices,
which we offer you firstly for you holy catholic Church.
Be pleased to grant her peace,
to guard, unite, and govern her throughout the whole world,
together with your servant N. our pope and N. our bishop,
and all those who, holding to the truth,
hand on the catholic and apostolic faith.

From the Canon of the Roman Missal

6

Review and Recommendations

PENTECOSTALISM AND THE VARIOUS charismatic movements' appeal and growth depends largely on how long they can sustain themselves in responding to the existential needs of contemporary middle-to-low income earners who are the majority in almost all of Africa's developing democracies. This situation calls for re-imagining a corollary—a social dimension where provision will be made for welfare and basic needs which many governments are unable to fulfill. This necessarily must put education, economy, health, opportunities, jobs, and general social welfare at the forefront of its evangelism. Pentecostals must also publicly denounce corruption in government, public, and private sectors. They must promote accountability of their own leaders and those in government. They must pay attention to opportunities for the children of poor members of their congregation. They also must work at dialogue and conflict resolution among the association of Christian bodies. It is sad that after four decades of phenomenal growth of Christianity on the African continent, endemic poverty and corruption still pervade the land. One then is forced to ask if the "Spirit-fired" preaching is unable to change hearts? Or are we to assume that the congregants hearts are focused on receiving their "break-throughs" without a call to conversion?

Neo-Pentecostalism in West Africa as a religious phenomenon is relatively young compared to its sister expression in Europe and America. It is still trying to find an adequate ecclesiology and theological foundation. Unfortunately, unlike its Western counterpart, African Pentecostalism is largely theologically unthematized.[1] Marius Nel, reflecting on the anti-intellectualism of South African Pentecostalism, opines that this is borne out of its poor and uneducated beginnings in which there was a literal reading and translation of the second coming of Christ, judgment, and heaven or hell. There was no necessity to waste time training. Nel avers, "Early Pentecostals also perceived that an intellectualisation of the Christian faith was resisting or even suppressing the work of the Holy Spirit, while the life of the spirit and the demands of intellectual labours were seen as opposites that do not readily mix."[2] Nel suggests that this anti-intellectualism rests on the observation that Pentecostal spirituality comes from affections, imagination, operating on the level of orality and daily "revelation" as opposed to intellectual logic and reason, written discourse, and argumentations on the nature of truth. However, Nel is quick to point out (and I am in agreement with him), "Contemporary Pentecostalism is neither anti-intellectual nor intellectual; both elements are present among Pentecostals worldwide . . . Pentecostal theological scholarship experiences to a certain extent tension with intellectual strains within Pentecostalism."[3] This I find to be true of how Pentecostal preachers relate with each other especially in Nigeria, Ghana, and Ivory Coast. There is a very gray line that separates Pentecostal pastors with some kind of higher degree or intellectual achievement from the pastor without any. Nel continues, "Pentecostal theological scholarship can rather be described in terms of affective and embodied epistemology, a holistic spirituality, and a non-reductionistic worldview as a criticism on what it perceieved as the pretentiousness of the scientific mind."[4]

There are a varied number of reasons why Pentecostalism needs to reinvent a theologically trained and thematized clergy, as well as facts of Pentecostal ecclesiology. Chief among these reasons include coherence, order, teaching structure, but above all, that people are not misled by unfounded teachings based on interpretations cooked up in personal and oftentimes twisted minds. There is an absolute and urgent need within contemporary Pentecostalism, especially in developing nations where there are more Pentecostal assemblies withn a radius of ten city blocks than there are grocery stores, office spaces, or empowerment agencies. In Nigeria, within the last

1. Rausch. "Catholics and Pentecostals," 937.
2. Nel, "Rather Spirit-Filled," 7.
3. Nel, "Rather Spirit-Filled," 9.
4. Nel, "Rather Spirit-Filled," 9.

twenty to thirty years, there are more "reverends" and "pastors" than there are any other professional titles in the public workspace.

Thomas Rausch draws a distinction when he averred,

> Until recently the majority of Pentecostal pastors have not had formal theological training. Prizing the priesthood of all believers and the Spirit's empowerment, Pentecostals prepare charismatic leaders as pastors through apprenticeship, without long educational programs in seminaries or accredited Bible institutes; this helps explain the remarkable ability of the movement to rapidly plant new churches. Today this pattern is changing. Classical Pentecostalism has developed its own academic societies, journals, and a new generation of Pentecostal and Charismatic academics who struggle to integrate critical exegesis, academic theology, and social concerns into the life of their churches without succumbing to a Western rationalism that loses a sense for the pneumatological. Many of these scholars suggest that Pentecostal theology in this new century needs to be 'contextualized.'[5]

A consideration for theological training, apologetics, critical studies of biblical texts within its historical and cultural contexts, the study of dogma, and the history of the Christian church: all of these polemicals can enhance the message of Pentecostal and charismatic movements. It is only when these studies encounter logical, contextual, and creative thinking that the claim to a Spirit-led worship can become aware of the social demands of justice and fair play. Frank Macchia argues that for Pentecostal spirituality to become liberating in a social ccontext, there will be a need to move from "a theology of 'Biblical doctrines' to the 'rise of critical theology' which is prophetically concerned for personal; and social liberation."[6] Pamela Holmes brilliantly and succinctly summarizes the necessity for a Pentecostal hermeneutical crossover in her work, stating,

> Although overcoming kyriarchical attitudes and practices with Pentecostalism will not be easy, it is possible. Pentecostals are intensely interested in liberation, in life abundant for *all*. There is an underlying, emancipatory impulse in Pentecostalism dating from its origins. Its continuing growth among oppressed, marginalized peoples continues to be fertile ground for this liberative lens. Today Pentecostalism is in position to reclaim its liberative stance and explicitly and intentionally reapply such a stance to all those

---

5. Rausch, "Catholics and Pentecostals," 937.
6. Dempster, Klaus, and Petersen, *Globalization of Pentecostalism*, 8–9.

within its own midst who are experiencing oppression, not only at the hands of others, but also as a sresult of its unacknowledged harmful, ideological presuppositions and its incongruent hermeneutical practices.[7]

One of the most dangerous aspects of religious beliefs is to give a false interpretation of the sacred texts and practices of a religion. While extremism or fanaticism is one thing, false teaching can enslave a people and make them slaves of devious creation of idols totally different from the gospel news of and about Christ. In cases like this, the attack on the human person is not from outside, rather, it comes from within. False religion by false teachers all through human history has led in only one direction: death. Jim Jones and the Guyana tragedy comes to mind. Bernard Leeming describes two formidable problems which exist and are easily used to hinder a possible unity of the churches, especially in the area of common worship or inter-ecclesial communion. First, there is a doctrinal fence which makes Catholic doctrines "human thinking," and oftentimes, Pentecostals claim these doctrines are not scriptural. On the part of Catholics weighing in, the doctrines of the church are backed by Scriptures, tradition, and magisterial authority of a long and distinguished, prayerful, and intellectual discernment.[8] Founders and general overseers determine what basic Pentecostalism teachings to follow. There are open-ended questions that need answering but the answers are not forthcoming so far:

- Does the Pentecostal church believe in the creed of the Christian church?
- If it does not, does this include or exclude them as a Christian church?
- Who detrmines managerial, structural, and clerical offices and promotions?
- What is the organizational structure of the enterprise in terms of discipline, the control of finances, a case of dissent, and schism?
- What is the evangelical concentration of the Pentecostal assemblies: urban, rural, churched, or unchurched people?
- What happens in the generation after the demise of the founding pastor?

---

7. Hunter and Ormerod, *The Many Faces*, 284–85.
8. Bea, *Unity of Christians*, 20.

Review and Recommendations

Some of the scholars who have undertaken indepth studies of Pentecostalism present some key theological differences which do not only hamper ecumenical dialogue, but enable mistrust and mutual suspicion to thrive. Some of these theological differences are:

1. Traditional Christian churches tend to stress an ecclesiology of continuity from the early church of the apostles, (as it was discussed extensively in the previous chapter), with a continous transmission of faith, sacraments, authority, and order. When placed against the restorationist claims of the Pentecostals, a problem here exists. The Pentecostals borrow from the Anabaptists who make the claim that the post-Constantine church had broken down, thus needing restoration based solely on the "New Testament" church.

2. While the traditional churches emphasize sacramental baptism by water, which includes the gift of the Spirit on the newly baptized, the Pentecostals emphasis Spirit baptism. This is accompanied by charismata, especially the gift of tongues. The argument for the traditional baptism, as it is found in Jesus' teaching in New Testament, and Spirit baptism, based on events in the early church of the apostles found in the Book of Acts, presents a dichotomy that needs theological reformation and resolution.

3. The ministerial offices in the traditional churches is a point of contention for the Pentecostal. The understanding of apostolicity in the Catholic Church, for instance, is perceived as the visible and unbroken connection in the ordination rite of the laying on of hands that goes back to the apostles. The authority of the ordained resides in the episcopal office. However, the Pentecostals percieve apostolicity as spiritual and invisble, which is found in the holiness of members and in the oneness of the assembly as a spiritual union. Rausch states that for Pentecostals, apostolicity implies the restoration of the apostolic gifts of the New Testatment churches which includes charismata. This, Rausch claims, is testimony to the Spirit's activity in the world.[9]

4. While the Orthodox and confessional older churches celebrate traditon in their ecumenical creed, sacraments, and the teachings handed on through the different ages of the church, pre- and post-Reformation, the Pentecostals are not in agreement that the formulation

---

9. Rausch, "Catholics and Pentecostals," 941.

of creeds are on a par with sacred Scripture. Rausch argues that "It is difficult for the Catholic Church to recognize "church" in the full sense in a community that does not understand the Eucharist as it was understood in the great tradition."[10]

5. The question of the primacy and infallibility of the pope remains a major defined doctrinal point. And even though the older tradition Christian churches have made some progress with the Pentecostals, the responses are different from one community to the other. The sacraments, especially the real presence of the Lord in the Eucharist, oracular confession, and absolution by a priest remains hotly contested, especially by Pentecostals (many of whom were practicing Catholics before their "conversion"). It is also argued that devotion to the blessed mother of God in any form is perceived by non-Catholics as idolatry. Interestingly, among a few AICs, we now find a growing body of devotion to the blessed Virgin Mary, which includes praying the holy rosary and seeking her intercession.

Outside of the Catholic Church and the churches that came out of the Reformation, most of the other Christian churches do not have a central teaching authority. The Roman Church gives credence to magisterial authority, the teaching office which maintains fidelity to apostolic tradition. As the Pentecostal churches continue to grow and expound, the necessity for articulating a theologically thought out doctrinal statement will become all too obvious. The claim can be made that the teaching authority of the church is always under the guidance of the Holy Spirit, therefore as Pentecostals centered on pneumatology, articulating a Pentecostal teaching authority should not be a difficult feat.[11] The necessity also for the Pentecostal fellowship to have a visible and viable unity *ad intra* makes ecumenical

---

10. Rausch, "Catholics and Pentecostals," 942.

11. In Bernard Leeming's work, he accentuates the importance of hierarchical order and discipline, especially when it comes to the doctrines and revealed truths. For Leeming, right from the apostles, the faithful transmission of what the Lord taught and handed on for their commission must be adhered to. In the writer's words, "With good reason the authority of the Church is vigilant about correct doctrine and about the protection of the faithful from dangerous influences. Rightly too, the Church regulates meetings and conversations with those of other communions on doctrinal questions. Even in discussions and collaboration with non-Catholics in matters not directly religious, for example, in questions of social work and relief, the faithful are warned not to do anything that would compromise revealed doctrine or the general outlook of the Church." Bea, *Unity of Christians*, 25.

dialogue easier *ad extra,* since our dialogue then will be more like families having a conversation than a heated town hall meeting.

CONCLUSION

If Africa will embrace its next historical phase as the new face of global Christianity, the ethics of Christian righteousness must shine forth equally out of Africa. In various ways, the older generations of traditional Christians born of the missionary enterprise have influenced social and cultural growth of many nation-states on the continent. The new Pentecostal phenomenon also continues to play its role in the political, economic, and social transformation of Africa. This research shows clearly that, at this time, there is no cohesive ecumenical interaction between traditional mainline Christian churches and the Pentecostal assemblies. Even though burgeoning numbers are on the side of Christianity in Africa, Africa's internecine, fratricidal wars, corrupt governments/leadership, and abject poverty are not abating—rather, they continue to grow. In some instances, some of the fraudulently set up "Pentecostal ministries," as found in many cities in West Africa, are complicit and major players in the racketeering, bankrupting, and bastardizing of many societies on the verge of total collapse. It cannot be overemphasized that African Christianity must unite in a fraternal ecumenical embrace to be midwives of new African democratic reconstruction, transition, and survival. This new Christian faith must work for and support new leaders who are altruistic, patriotic, and persons of integrity. They must be at the forefront of mediation between many conflicting African countries or ethnic divides. Many pulpits can become a veritable tool for national, social consciousness and the reconstruction of new nations from the battered and previously crumbled ones.

I find Wolfgang Vondey's conclusion instructive and useful for my own summary where he sees a necessary interdependence between ecumenism and Pentecostalism in contemporary times. According to Vondey, "The future of ecumenical conversations with Pentecostals does not lie in a numerical growth of the number of bilateral dialogues, although this is desirable. Most important is the transformation of the existing status quo, including the provision of new and unprecedented opportunities, structures, and procedures for initiating ecumenical encounter and sustaining ecumenical relationships among churches and communities that do not always possess a solid footing in the historical traditions of Christendom."[12] For Vondey, some level of ecumenical unity must be achieved to avoid the continuous presentation of a diverse and global puzzle of visually divided churches.

It is sad but clearly true that ecumenism is not about a possible re-unification of divisions and deep separations caused by schisms; notwithstanding, for Christianity to remain a global force for good, there is a need to come together in a fraternal ecumenical unity to renew Africa and the world. Perhaps then, African Christianity can become missionaries to the world. Hollenweger warns,

> Either the Christians are successful in finding a new unity, which is not based (or at least not entirely based) on the traditions of the West and its organizational models, or we will face a split in Christianity that will have more painful consequences than the split between Catholics and Protestants. It will be a split that strengthens the already existing political and economic antagonism between the north and the south. Such development would contradict the very essence of twentieth century ecumenism. It can only be avoided if we resolutely develop tools for the forging of *an intercultural theology*[13] that will not be conceptually uniform but still nevertheless provide the basis for a mutual recognition and a global learning process. Such an intercultural theology would have to make use of, parabolic, dramatic and narrative patterns and shift the emphasis from the debate of conceptual consensus statements to the exploration and identification of those questions that matter for our cultural, spiritual and physical survival. Such a theology would not rule out the use of Mediterranean European categories but their use would not be governed entirely by faithfulness to the historical heritage but equally by commitment to the vital issues of our time.[14]

Gosbert Byamungu's reflections add voice to ways by which Pentecostalism with its numbers can be a tool for social engagement in the political landscape of Africa. According to Byamungu, we must first acknowledge that these many varied and rival denominations on the continent are not due the original *faux pas* of missionary enterprise. Byamungu argues that it is necessary to admit that "Africa has consciously, or unconsciously, uncritically

---

12. Robeck Jr. and Yong, *Cambridge Companion*, 288.
13. Emphasis is mine.
14. Hollenweger, "After Twenty Years' Research," 12.

perpetuated the inherited divisions and indeed that it continues to take initiatives to multiply them. It is possible to argue that these divisions are maintained because of interests beyond the gospel."[15] Byamungu opines that access to amenities provided by the missionaries, not the discovery of the truth about Jesus and his gospel, divided the pioneering African Christians. He states that now that Africans understand the Bible and know Jesus and his gospel, "it is high time to purify our intentions in embracing the gospel of love and unity, and not for the sake of eschatological salvation, but concretely also for the fullness of life here and now. For both objectives unity is imperative, and division is dysfunctional."[16] Therefore, for an ecumenism that can lead to social action on behalf of the poor, Byamungu proposes a few "*African*" models to help;

- There is a need to return to the very heart of Africa and our "*Africanness*," which is oneness of community. This is a value inherent to the fundamental identity of the African people. This rapprochement is gold for African ecumenism. The natural African propensity towards dialogue is the fundamental one which African Christianity must dig deeply and base its ecumenical unity on.

- The traditional African concept of religion is another model worth examining closely. For the African, religion is an ontological reality, which marks one's life from cradle to the grave. Religion as cultic practices and worship of the gods build communities and not tear them apart. Peaceful co-existence in religious pluralism is a lesson for current African Christianity.

- Africa's diverse and multi-cultural plurality is a microcosm of an essential cultural plurality that exists within the universal church. This

---

15. Byamungu, "Construing Newer 'Windows,'" 346. In Byamungu's reflections, he clarifies further, "Early Christian missionary activity was more directed towards saving souls than towards enhancing the material wellbeing and welfare of the people. As a result, and applying the worldly orientation of traditional African religion, it was not perceived as particularly relevant, since the people did not doubt their own spirituality. Later orientations, which associated the Christian mission with education, health services, and the overarching goal of 'progress' or development, provided concrete incentives for potential converts . . . Missionary activity, apart from the preaching of the gospel, had to adopt a technique of proselytizing either by persuasion or by coercion. Persuasion went hand in hand with certain benefits to be had through adhesion to the particular mission that was offering them. This was important for 'conversion', the school, the hospital, the job." Byamungu, "Construing Newer 'Windows,'" 347.

16. Byamungu, "Construing Newer 'Windows,'" 347.

is an important reality for ecumenism in Africa, "to recognize that Africa is diverse, that our Church traditions and practices will therefore be diverse even as they reflect this vastness of the continent and the plurality of our cultures. This call for an ecumenism that takes account of this cross-cultural penetration and counter penetration, and that may not seek a uniformity which can only be artificial and dysfunctional."[17]

- To re-evaluate the past mistakes made by post-independent Christianity, where traditional religions were vilified and demonized as pagan and heathen, it is important to probe the traditional African value system, which engendered peaceful co-existence, unity, solidarity, and rapprochement.

- To call to mind that the suffering of the churches in "the two-thirds world becomes a *locus theologicus* . . . emphasizing that its ministry of the word and sacraments can only be convincing if it actively engages in economic and all human development, struggling for justice and peace in the world as a whole."[18]

Byamungu surmises that "Christianities" in Africa necessarily must find ways to unite ecumenically and present one front, rich diversities of expression, vibrant in cultural life existing in a caring and healing dynamism. Byamungu warns, "Denominationalism and sectarianism weaken the strength of the gospel and its spirituality, and annul its kerygmatic potential. Its disunity and petty competitions weaken its power to face the challenges of pluralism, especially where other religions propose their programs of liberating the poor."[19] These models proposed by Byamungu remain an essential aspect of the ecumenical breakdown between the Pentecostal assemblies and the traditional Christian churches, Orthodox, or traditional African impulses.

When all of these facts are taken into consideration, one cannot but submit that the fragmentation and continuous, seemingly endless proliferation of the body of Christ continues to call for concern. It is clear that the unity of Christ's followers is imperiled by humanity's greed, pride, search for power, and the lack of good will and humility to wash each others' feet. The necessity for unity clearly does not include the reunification of

---

17. Byamungu, "Construing Newer 'Windows,'" 349.
18. Byamungu, "Construing Newer 'Windows,'" 349–50.
19. Byamungu, "Construing Newer 'Windows,'" 351.

different Christian groups into one universal Christian church under any agreeable guise. However, ecumenism must be preserved if only for the preservation and protection of the Christian faith. At this time in human history, Christianity and Christians continues to be the most persecuted religious practice in the world. Most of the liberal world's moral and ethical changes directly are in contradiction with traditional Christian teachings. The continuous splintering of Christianity does not help Christianity, but adds to the damage years of schisms and separation has caused.

Not to sound pessimistic, haughty, or triumphalistic, I cannot help myself from the feeling of frustration, sadness, and anger I have when I see self-appointed, self-acclaimed, and self-consecrated "clerics." Perhaps part of what vexes me so is seeing these gatherings of tens of thousands of religious voyeurists and miracle seekers been fleeced by con artists, wolves in sheep's clothing. It may not be far from the truth that I dislike the opulence of modern day mega-televangelists, preachers, and motivational speakers for twisting sacred Scripture and using the gospel, force-fitting it into a consumer good to earn tithes, seeds sown, and to keep laughing to their foreign banks at the expense of a people already subjugated and beaten into the ground by a system endemically corrupt. Yet, in this direst of situation, the words of Innocent Onyewuenyi encourages us still,

> Ecumenism is a sign of atonement for regrettable acts on both sides; it is a manifestation of a determination to construct together, in obedience to the Lord, a new era of brotherhood; it is living once more for the greater good of souls and the coming of the kingdom; it is setting free so many hearts which had been prisoners of their bitterness, locked in reciprocal distrust; it is all of us at the same moment hearing the voice of the Lord asking each of us "where is your brother?"; it is beginning to look for one another and finally meeting as brothers.[20]

We must all submit that Christ will give life to his church till the end of time for those who worship in Spirit and in truth. The Spirit that gives life must lead all of us to he who is the way, the *truth*, and life.

---

20. Onyewuenyi, "Ecumenism," 167–71.

Appendix A
Figures

FIGURE 1: DISTRIBUTION OF SURVEY PARTICIPANTS BY COUNTRY SEX AND AGE GROUP

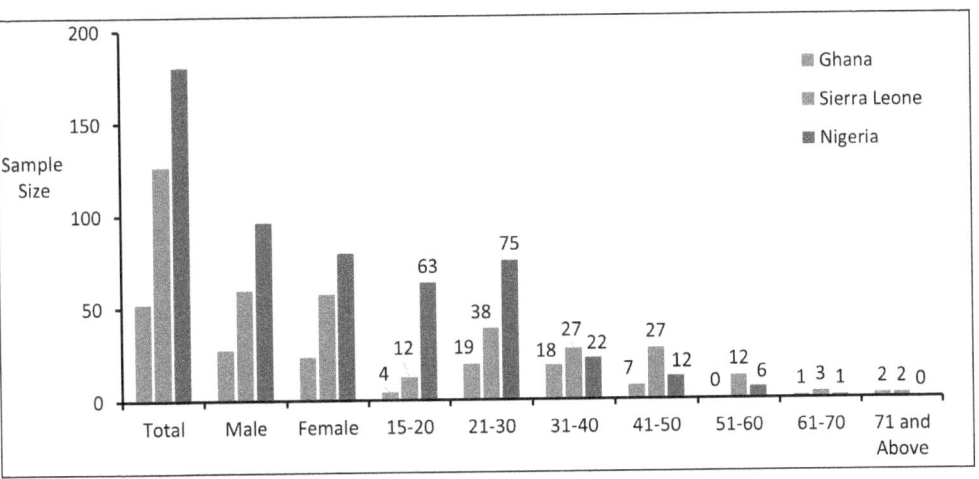

Appendix A

TABLE 1: NUMBER OF PARTICIPANTS GROUPED BY THEIR COUNTRY

Location	Ghana	Sierra Leone	Nigeria	Total
Male	27	59	96	182
Female	23	57	79	159
No response (male female)	2	10	5	17
15-20	4	12	63	79
21-30	19	38	75	132
31-40	18	27	22	67
41-50	7	27	12	46
51-60	0	12	6	18
61-70	1	3	1	5
71 and Above	2	2	0	4
No response (age group)	1	5	1	7
Total Sample Size	52	126	180	358

Figures

FIGURE 2: RESPONSE ON RELIGIOUS AFFILIATIONS FROM BIRTH, AT AND BEFORE CONVERSION, GROUPED BY COUNTRY

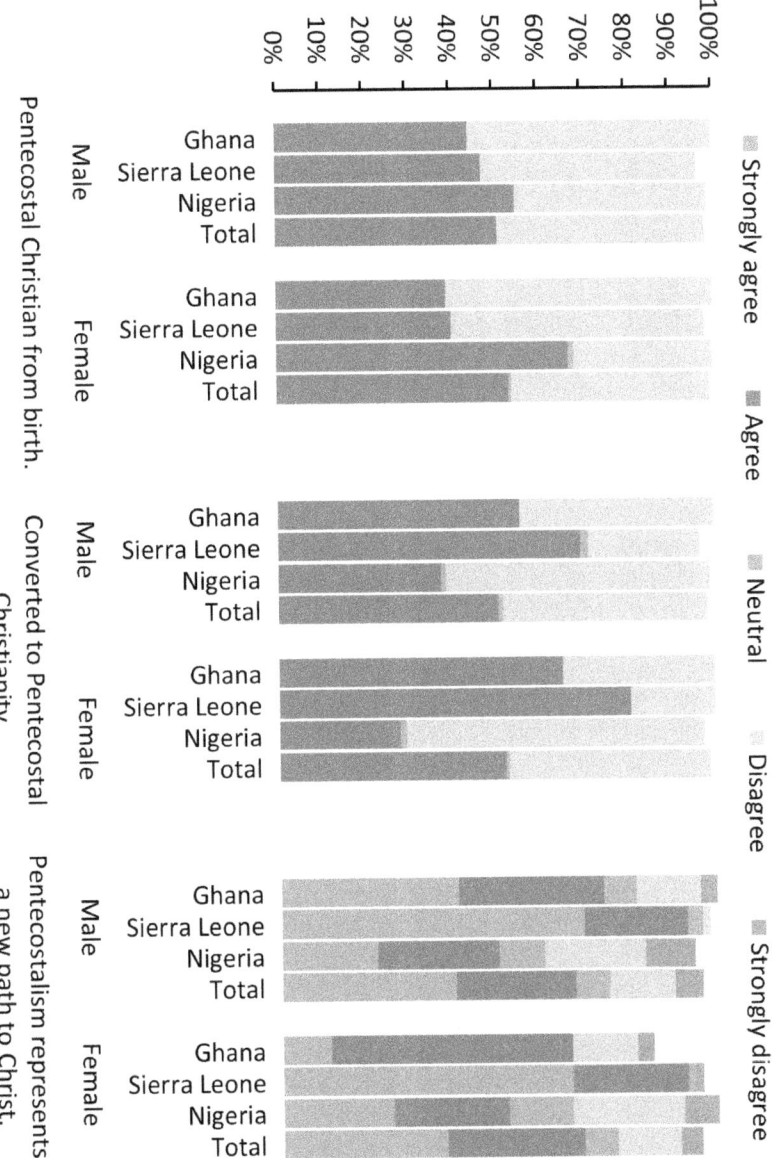

Appendix A

FIGURE 3: RESPONSE ON RELIGIOUS AFFILIATIONS FROM BIRTH, AT AND BEFORE CONVERSION, GROUPED BY COUNTRY AND AGE GROUP

Pentecostals: Previous religious affiliation

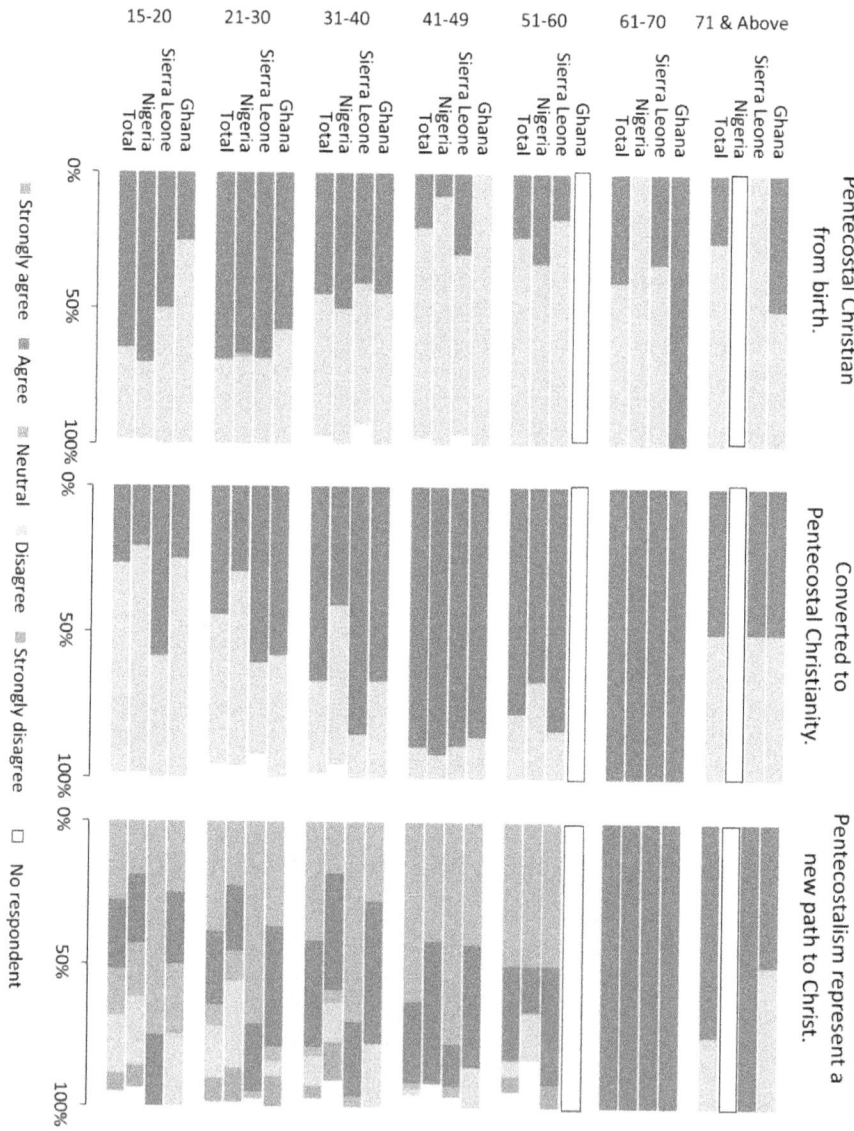

FIGURE 4: PREVIOUS RELIGIOUS AFFILIATIONS BEFORE CONVERSION, GROUPED BY COUNTRY, SEX AND AGE GROUP

Others: Muslim, Celestial Church of Christ, CAC, Apostolic Church, Cherubim and Seraphim, Baptist, Jehovah's Witnesses, Seventh-day Adventist, Deeper Life Bible Church

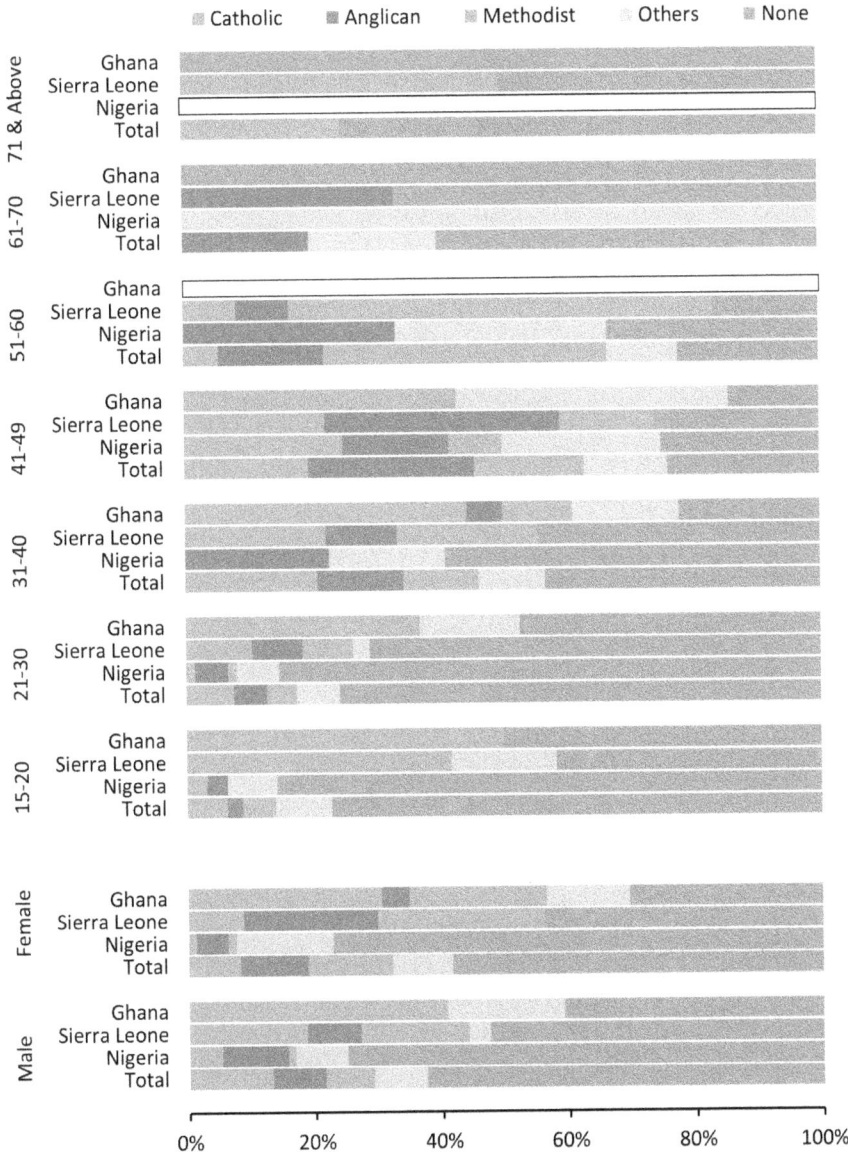

Appendix A

FIGURE 5: TRADITIONAL CHRISTIAN TIES GROUPED BY COUNTRY AND SEX

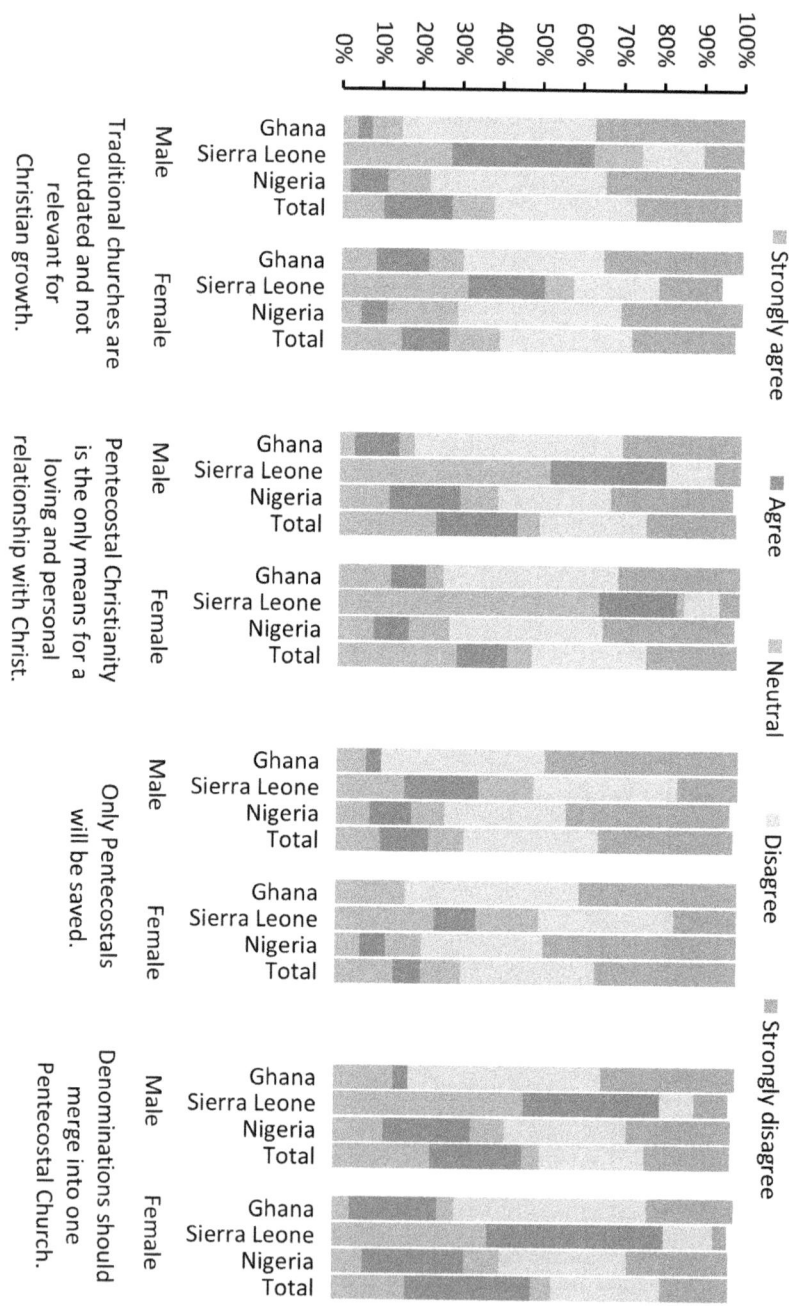

FIGURE 6: TRADITIONAL CHRISTIAN TIES GROUPED BY COUNTRY AND AGE GROUP

Christian Traditions

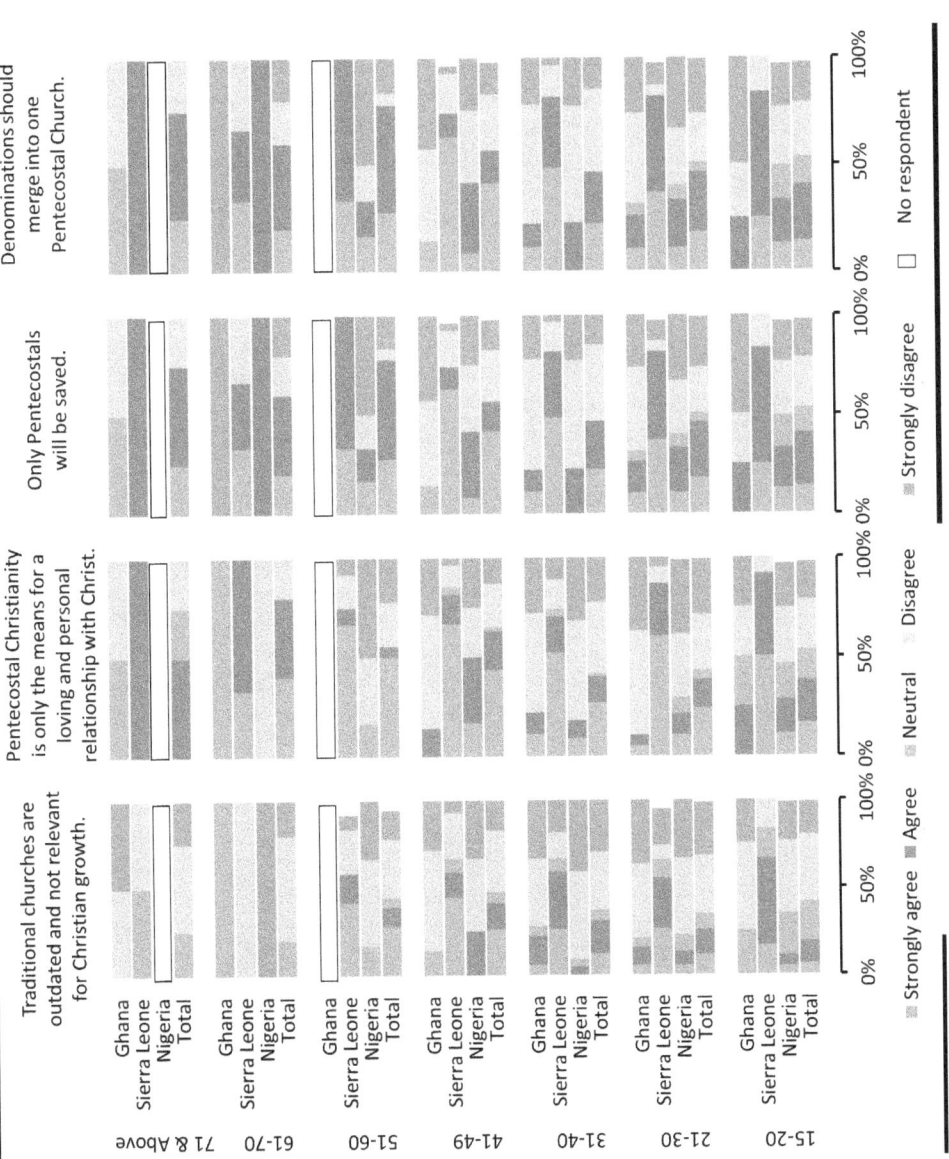

Appendix A

FIGURE 7: RESPONSE ON CHRISTIAN TRADITIONS GROUPED BY COUNTRY AND SEX

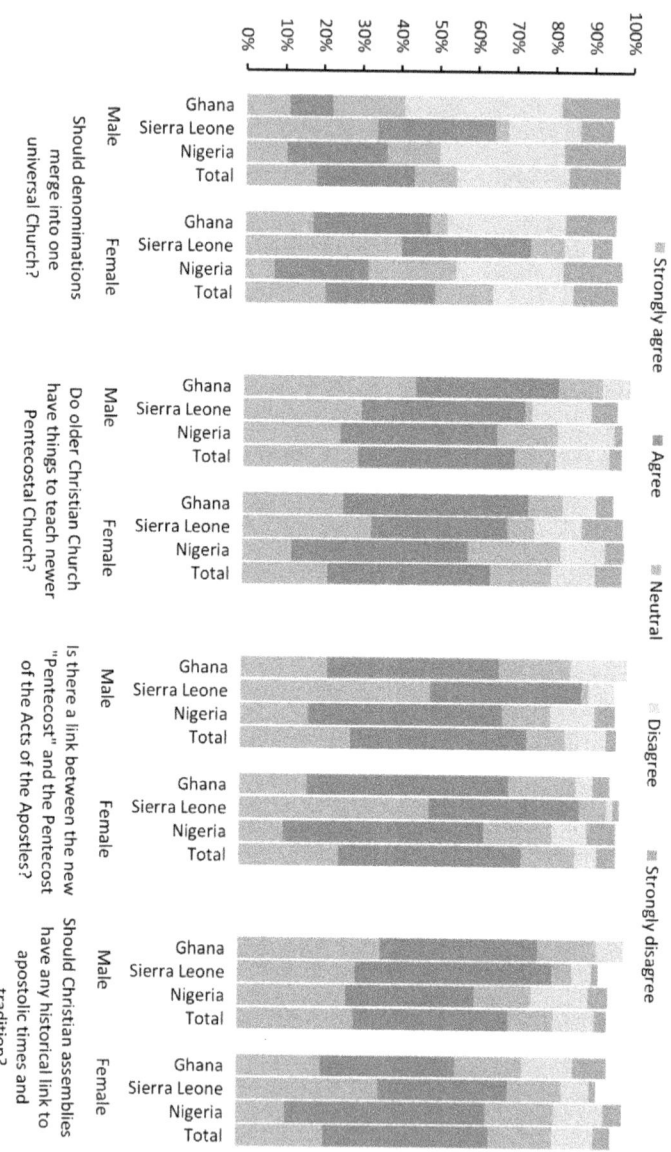

Figures

FIGURE 8: RESPONSE ON CHRISTIAN TRADITIONS GROUPED BY COUNTRY AND AGE GROUP

Social condition of Christians

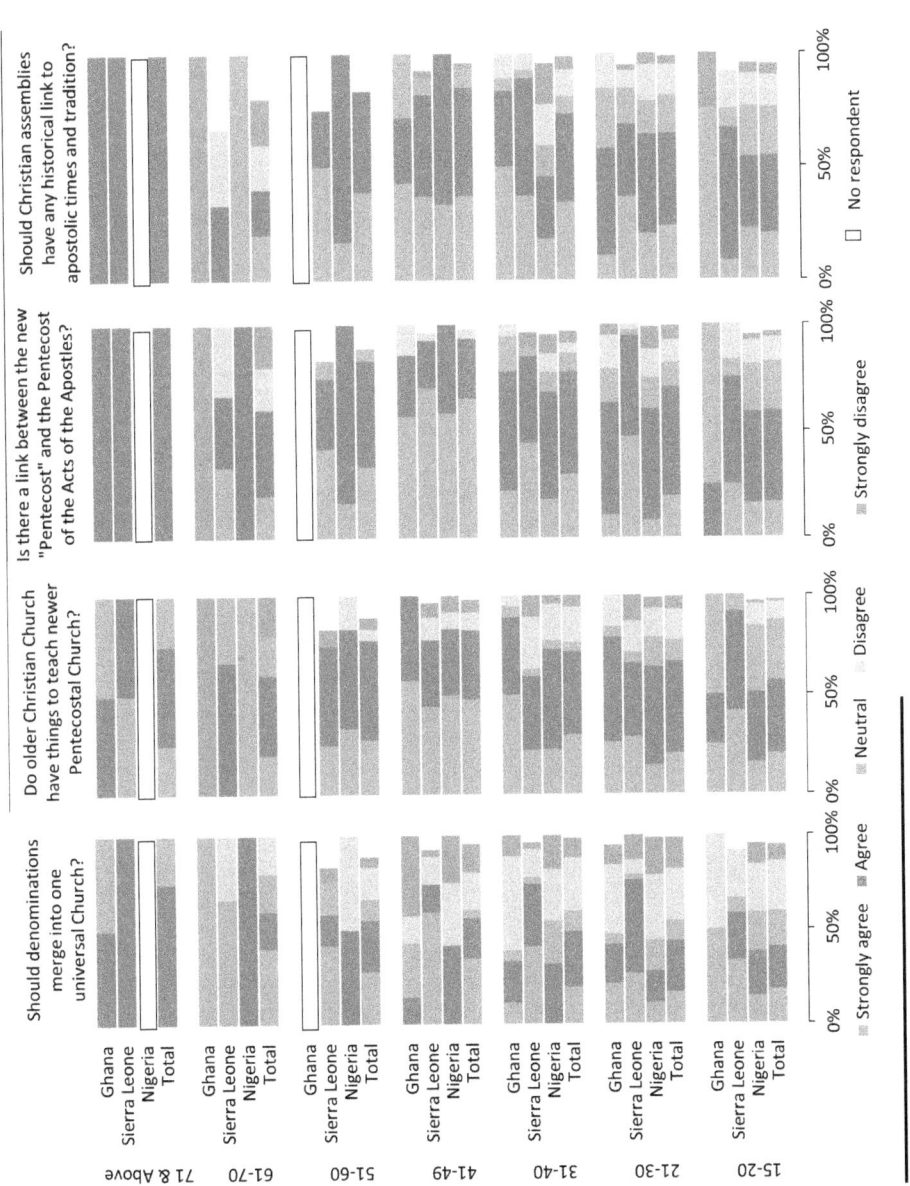

Appendix A

FIGURE 9: DO YOU AGREE THAT CHRISTIAN COMMUNITIES SHOULD PLAY AN ACTIVE SOCIAL ROLE IN THE SOCIETY?

Ecumenism

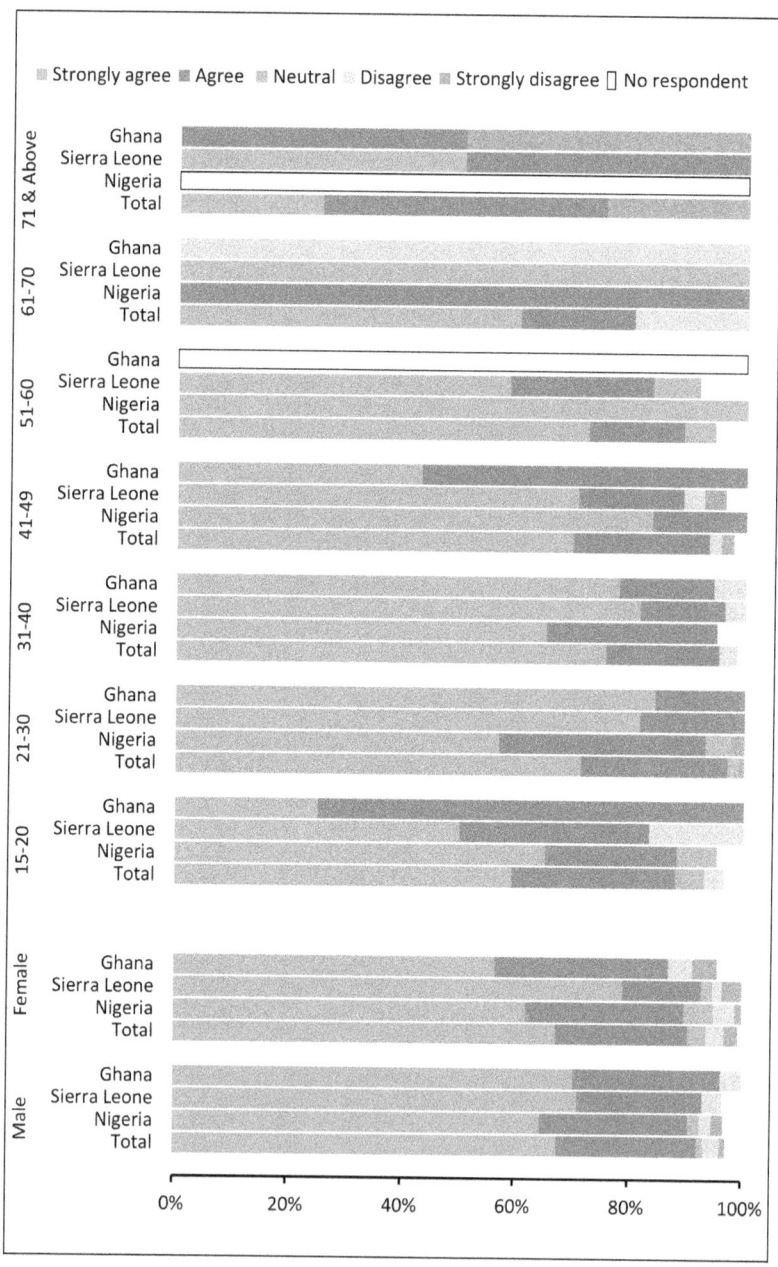

FIGURE 10: RESPONSE ON CHRISTIAN ECUMENISM GROUPED BY COUNTRY AND SEX

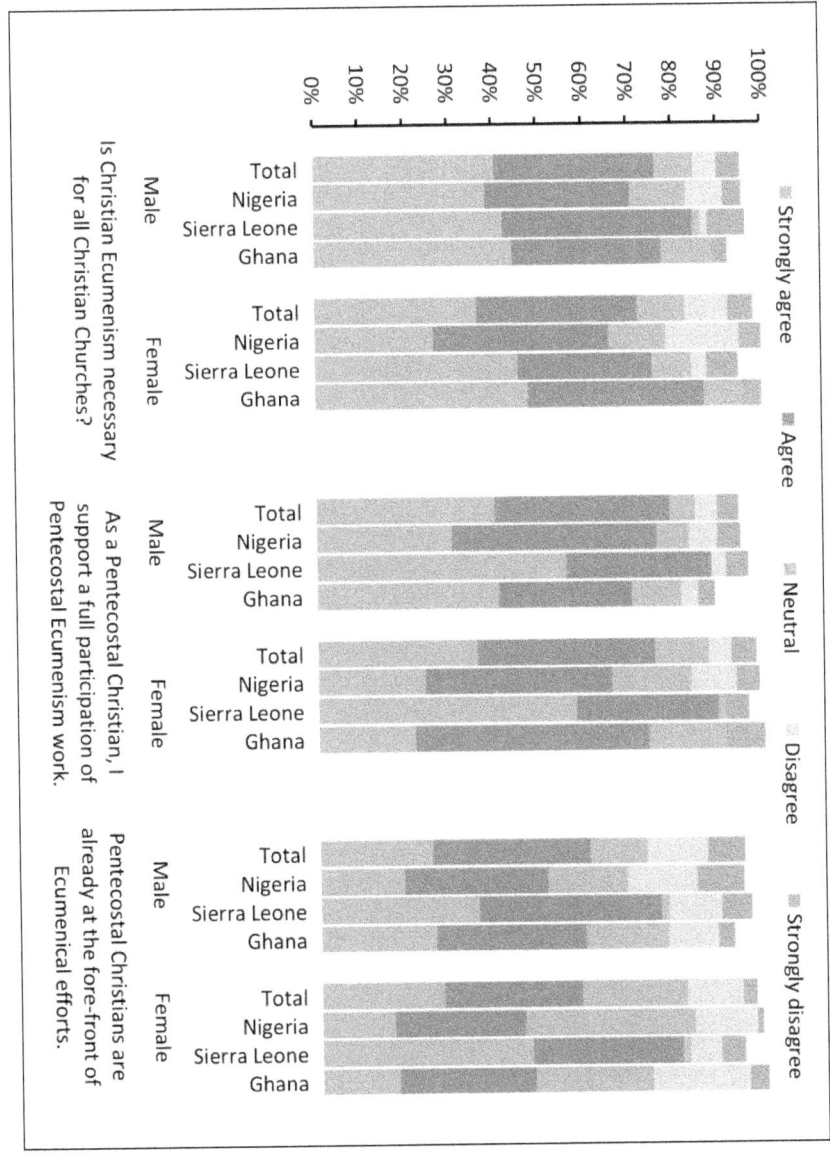

Appendix A

FIGURE 11: RESPONSE ON CHRISTIAN ECUMENISM GROUPED BY COUNTRY AND AGE GROUP

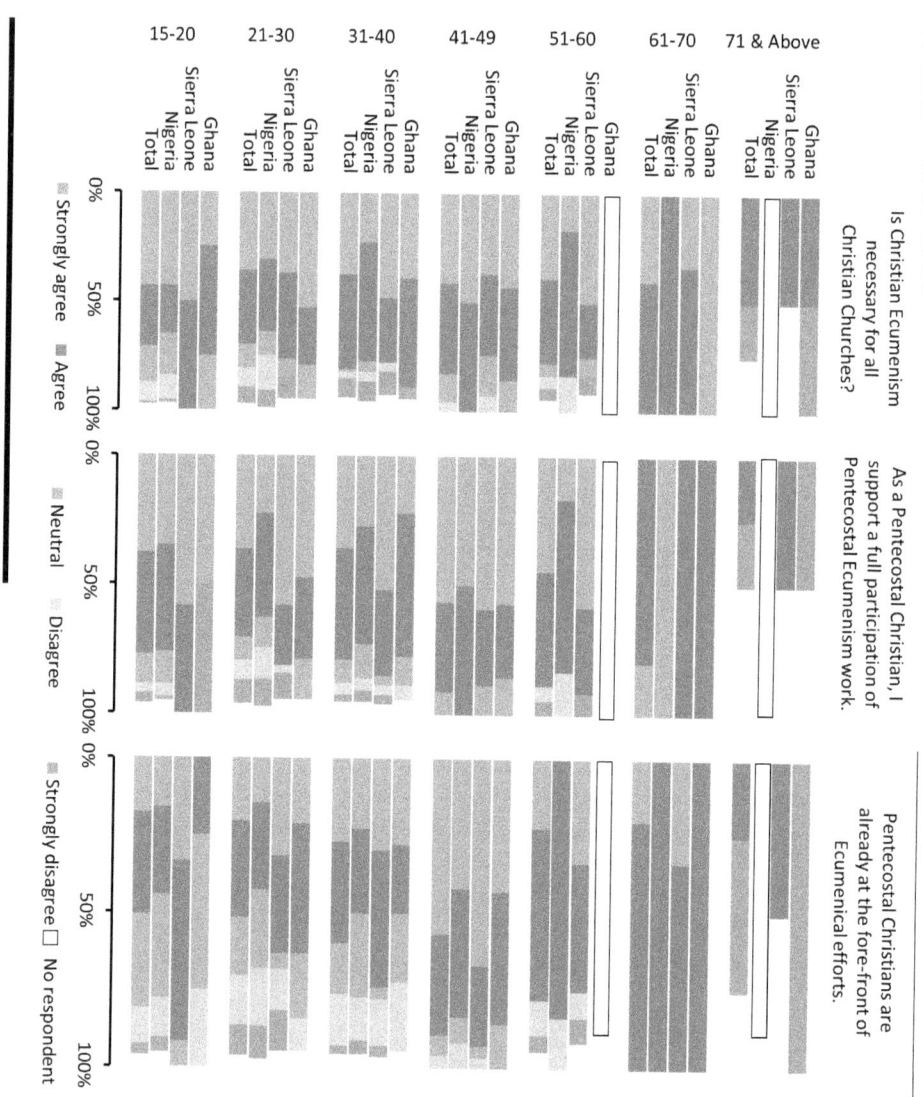

Appendix B
Sample Questionnaires I & II

PASTORS'/GOS' QUESTIONNAIRE

1. What are the factor(s) that led you to a personal call to find a church/Christian community?
2. In the light of this call/vocation, how do you respond to and understand Jesus' prayer for the unity of his body in John's gospel? (John 17:20–23)
3. In what ways do you understand Christian ecumenical efforts?
4. Do you see any necessity for ecumenical work among the various churches?
5. In what ways do you think dialogue within the churches should proceed, and what objectives should they strive to achieve?
6. What do you perceive to be the reason(s) for the division(s) that sets Pentecostalism apart from the older Christian traditions?
7. What do you suppose are the attractions of Pentecostalism which account for its current appeal and its numerical strength?
8. What will you consider the basic foundations of Pentecostal evangelism, mission, and ministry?
9. How do Pentecostals understand authority, clerical order, and discipline in their governing structure?
10. Do you think Pentecostalism is a passing phenomenon as some say, or a "new Pentecost" and renewal of the churches into the future?

Thank you for your time and participation.
Rev. Dr. John Segun Odeyemi

Appendix B

CHRISTIAN ECUMENISM AND PENTECOSTALISM IN WEST AFRICA: A TEMPLATE FOR A GLOBAL PHENOMENON

Questionnaire

NB: This questionnaire seeks to investigate and study how congregants at Pentecostal churches/faith communities understand ecumenical work as a common front for the Christian churches, and to inquire if it is perceived to be of any necessity. This "common front" should not be understood as a merger of all communities of faith into one universal church. Rather, it should be seen as a call for a closer confession of faith in Christ and an attempt at a unilateral action to disavow social and economic, unjust and corrupt structures in developing democracies, especially of the Global South. The questions are designed to be easily understood and there are five options to answer from. After the collation of responses, this questionnaire will be a big part of a proposed upcoming book publication. Thank you for your participation, Blessings, grace, and peace be with you.

Participants' Info:

Male [ ] Female [ ]

Age Range: 15–20 [ ] 21–30 [ ] 31–40 [ ] 41–50 [ ] 51–60 [ ] 61–70 [ ] 71 and above [ ]

Student [ ] Secondary [ ] Higher Education [ ] Working Class [ ] Retiree [ ]

Nationality:

I am a Pentecostal Christian from birth.

1. Strongly Agree [ ]
2. Agree [ ]
3. Strongly Disagree [ ]
4. Disagree [ ]
5. Undecided [ ]

I was converted to Pentecostal Christianity.

1. Strongly Agree [ ]
2. Agree [ ]
3. Strongly Disagree [ ]
4. Disagree [ ]
5. Undecided [ ]

[NB: Please state what your religious affiliation was before your conversion, i.e., Catholic, Anglican, Methodist, etc._____.]

In your experience, does Pentecostalism represent a new path to Christ?

1. Strongly Agree [ ]
2. Agree [ ]
3. Strongly Disagree [ ]
4. Disagree [ ]
5. Undecided [ ]

Do you agree with the claim that the traditional Christian churches (Catholics, Anglicans, Methodists, etc) are outdated, dead in the Spirit, and no longer relevant for Christian growth?

1. Strongly Agree [ ]
2. Agree [ ]
3. Strongly Disagree [ ]
4. Disagree [ ]
5. Undecided [ ]

Appendix B

Do you believe that Pentecostal Christianity is the only sure means by which a Christian can form a loving and personal relationship with Christ?

1. Strongly Agree [ ]
2. Agree [ ]
3. Strongly Disagree [ ]
4. Disagree [ ]
5. Undecided [ ]

Do you believe that only Pentecostal Christians will be saved?

1. Strongly Agree [ ]
2. Agree [ ]
3. Strongly Disagree [ ]
4. Disagree [ ]
5. Undecided [ ]

If it is possible, do you think the existing denominations should merge into one Pentecostal church?

1. Strongly Agree [ ]
2. Agree [ ]
3. Strongly Disagree [ ]
4. Disagree [ ]
5. Undecided [ ]

Conversely, if it is possible, do you think the existing denominations should merge into one universal Christian church?

1. Strongly Agree [ ]
2. Agree [ ]
3. Strongly Disagree [ ]
4. Disagree [ ]
5. Undecided [ ]

Do you think that the Older Christian churches have things of Christian value to teach the newer Pentecostal churches?

1. Strongly Agree [ ]
2. Agree [ ]
3. Strongly Disagree [ ]
4. Disagree [ ]
5. Undecided [ ]

Do you see a link between this "new Pentecost" and the Pentecost in the Acts of the Apostles?

1. Strongly Agree [ ]
2. Agree [ ]
3. Strongly Disagree [ ]
4. Disagree [ ]
5. Undecided [ ]

Appendix B

Do you perceive any kind of necessity for Christian assemblies to have any historical link to apostolic times and tradition?

1. Strongly Agree [ ]
2. Agree [ ]
3. Strongly Disagree [ ]
4. Disagree [ ]
5. Undecided [ ]

Do you agree that Christian communities should play an active social role in society?

1. Strongly Agree [ ]
2. Agree [ ]
3. Strongly Disagree [ ]
4. Disagree [ ]
5. Undecided [ ]

Christian ecumenism (presenting a common front in the confession of faith and response to the world) is necessary for all Christian churches.

1. Strongly Agree [ ]
2. Agree [ ]
3. Strongly Disagree [ ]
4. Disagree [ ]
5. Undecided [ ]

As a Pentecostal Christian, I support a full participation of Pentecostals in ecumenical work.

1. Strongly Agree [ ]
2. Agree [ ]
3. Strongly Disagree [ ]
4. Disagree [ ]
5. Undecided [ ]

Pentecostal Christians are already at the forefront of ecumenical efforts.

1. Strongly Agree [ ]
2. Agree [ ]
3. Strongly Disagree [ ]
4. Disagree [ ]
5. Undecided [ ]

Bibliography

Abraham, Kuruvilla C. *Third World Theologies: Commonalities and Divergences.* Maryknoll, NY: Orbis, 1990.
Afolayan, Adesina, Olajumoke Yacob-Haliso and Toyin Falola, eds. *Pentecostalism and Politics in Africa.* Switzerland: Palgrave Macmillan/Springer Publishing, 2018.
Akinwale, Anthony A. and Joseph Kenny, eds. *Tradition and Compromises: Essays on the Challenge of Pentecostalism.* Ibadan, Nigeria: Dominican Institute, 2004.
Anderson, Allan, et al., eds. *Studying Global Pentecostalism: Theories and Methods.* Berkeley: University of California Press, 2010.
Anderson, Allan Heaton. *An Introduction to Pentecostalism: Global Charismatic Christianity.* 2nd ed. Cambridge, UK: Cambridge University Press, 2014.
Asamoah-Gyadu, K. "Missionaries without Robes: Lay Charismatic Fellowship and the Evangelization of Ghana." *Pneuma* 19 (1997) 167–88.
Bayart, J. F. *The State in Africa: Politics of Belly.* Harlow: Longman Publishing, 1995.
Bea, Augustine. *The Unity of Christians.* Edited by Bernard Leeming. Montreal: Palm Publishers, 1963.
Bediako, Kwame. *Christianity in Africa: The Renewal of a Non-Western Religion.* Edinburgh: Edinburgh University Press, 1995.
Bonny, Johan. "Perspectives on the Future of Ecumenism: The 50th Anniversary of Unitatis Redintegratio." *International Journal for the Study of the Christian Church* 15 (July 2015) 108–22.
Bräuer, Martin. "Pope Francis and Ecumenism." *The Ecumenical Review* 69 (March 2017) 4–14.
The Breviary, Vol. III. Dublin, Ireland: The Talbot Press, 1974.
Brie, Mircea. "Contemporary Ecumenism Between the Theologians Discourse and the Reality of Inter-Confessional Dialogue." *Journal for the Study of Religions and Ideologies* 8 (2009) 257–83.
Byamungu, Gosbert T. M. "Construing Newer 'Windows' of Ecumenism for Africa: A Catholic Perspective." *The Ecumenical Review* 53 (July 2001) 341–52.
Cardinal Onaiyekan, John, *Ecumenism and the Pentecostal Church in Nigeria Today*, in discussion with the author at the archbishop's house, Abuja, Nigeria, 2017.
Dempster, Murray W., Byron D. Klaus, and Douglas Petersen. *The Globalization of Pentecostalism: A Religion made to Travel.* Carlisle, CA: Regnum Books, 1999.
Duffy, Eamon. *Ten Popes Who Shook the World.* New Haven, CT: Yale University Press, 2011.

Bibliography

Faggioli, Massimo. *A Council for the Global Church: Receiving Vatican II in History*. Minneapolis: Augsburg, 2015.

Flannery, Austin. *Vatican Council II: Constitutions, Decrees, Declarations*. Vatican Collection. Northport, NY: Costello, 1996.

Gifford, Paul. *African Christianity: Its Public Role*. London: Hurst & Company, 1998.

Gros, Jeffrey. "Toward Full Communion: Faith and Order and Catholic Ecumenism." *Theological Studies* 65 (February 2004) 23–43.

Haight, Roger. "Responding to Fundamentalism in Africa: Three Questions for the Mainline Churches." *New Theology Review* 7 (1994) 5–13.

Haynes, J. *Religion and Politics in Africa*. London: Zed Books, 1996.

Hollenweger, Walter J. "After Twenty Years' Research on Pentecostalism." *International Review of Mission* 75 (January 1986) 3–12.

———. "After Twenty Years' Research on Pentecostalism." *Theology* 87 (November 1984) 403–12.

The Holy Bible. King James Version. New York: American Bible Society, 1999.

Hunter, Harold D. and Neil Ormerod. *The Many Faces of Global Pentecostalism*. Cleveland, TN: CPT Press, 2013.

Ibrahim, Ibrahim Yahaya. "The Wave of Jihadist Insurgency in West Africa: Global Ideology, Local Context, Individual Motivations." *West African Papers* 7 (August 2017).

Idowu, E. Bolaji. *African Traditional Religion: A Definition*. Maryknoll, NY; London: Orbis; SCM, 1973.

Ijezie, Luke Emehiele, Stephen Audu, and Agnes I. Acha. *The Church in Nigeria and Ecumenical Question*. Port Harcourt, Nigeria: CATHAN Publications, 2015.

Ishola, S. Ademola and Deji Ayegboyin. *Rediscovering and Fostering Unity in the Body of Christ: The Nigerian Experience*. Ibadan, Nigeria: Africa Theological Fellowship in association with Wellspring Publication, 2000.

Isichie, E. *A History of Christianity in Africa: From Antiquity to the Present*. London: SPCK, 1995.

Jones, Robert P., and Daniel Cox. "America's Changing Religious Identity: Findings from the 2016 American Values Atlas." *Research* (blog), PRRI, September 6, 2017, https://www.prri.org/research/american-religious-landscape-christian-religiously-unaffiliated/.

Kalu, Ogbu U. *African Pentecostalism: An Introduction*. Oxford, NY: Oxford University Press, 2008.

Kinnamon, Michael. *Signs of the Spirit: Official Report, Seventh Assembly, World Council of Churches Canberra, Australia*. Geneva; Grand Rapids: WCC Publications; Eerdmans, 1991.

Komonchak, Joseph A., Mary Collins, and Dermot A. Lane. *The New Dictionary of Theology*. Wilmington, DE: Michael Glazier, 1988.

Lowery, Mark D. *Ecumenism: Striving for Unity Amid Diversity*. Mystic, CT: Twenty-Third Publications, 1985.

Macchia, Frank D. "The Tongues of Pentecost: A Pentecostal Perspective on the Promise and Challenge of Pentecostal/Roman Catholic Dialogue." *Journal of Ecumenical Studies* 35 (1998) 1–18.

McBrien, Richard P. *Catholicism*. New York: Harper San Francisco, 1994.

McDonnell, Kilian. *Charismatic Renewal and Ecumenism*. New York: Paulist, 1978.

Bibliography

McManners, John. *The Oxford Illustrated History of Christianity*. Oxford, NY: Oxford University Press, 1990.

Meyer, Birgit. "Christianity in Africa: From African Independent to Pentecostal-Charismatic Churches." *Annual Review of Anthropology* 33 (2004) 447–74.

Müller, Johannes and Karl Gabriel. *Evangelicals, Pentecostal Churches, Charismatics: New Religious Movements as a Challenge for the Catholic Church*. Quezon City, Philippines: Claretian Communications Foundation, 2015.

Murray W. Dempster, Bryon D. Klaus, and Douglas Petersen, eds. *The Globalization of Pentecostalism: A Religion Made to Travel*. Carlisle, CA: Regnum Books, 1999.

N'Guessan, Konstanze. "Côte d'Ivoire: Pentecostalism, Politics, and Performances of the Past." *Nova Religio: The Journal of Alternative and Emergent Religions* 18 (2015) 80–100.

Ndiokwere, Nathaniel I. *The African Church, Today and Tomorrow (Vol. II), Prospects and Challenges*. Onitsha, Nigeria: Effective Key Publishers, 1994.

Nel, Marius. "Rather Spirit-Filled than Learned! Pentecostalism's Tradition of Anti-Intellectualism and Pentecostal Theological Scholarship." *Verbum et Ecclesia* 37 (May 2016) 1–9.

Odeyemi, John Segun. "Proclamation and Liberation as Models for a Post Synodal and Post Independent Churches in Africa: Re-Imagining the Possibilities in the Light of Pope Francis' Evangelii Gaudium." *The International Journal of African Catholicism* 9 (Winter 2017) 167–71.

Onyewuenyi, Innocent C. "Ecumenism: The Nigerian Context." *African Ecclesial Review* 20 (1979) 167–71.

Peel, J. D. Y. *Christianity, Islam, and Orisa Religion: Three Traditions in Comparison and Interaction*. Oakland: University of California Press, 2016.

Pillay, Jerry. "Ecumenism in Africa: Theological, Contextual, and Institutional Challenges." *The Ecumenical Review* 67 (December 2015) 635–50.

Pope Francis. *Pope Francis: Conversations with Jorge Bergoglio*. Edited by Sergio Rubin and Francesca Ambrogetti. New York: G.P. Putnam›s Sons, 2013.

Pope Francis. "Apostolic Exhortation: Evangelii Gaudium of the Holy Father Francis." *Apostolic Exhortations* (blog), *The Holy See*, 2013, http://w2.vatican.va/content/francesco/en/apost_exhortations/documents/papa-francesco_esortazione-ap_20131124_evangelii-gaudium.html.

Pope John Paul II. "Lettera Enciclica: Ut Unum Sint." *Encicliche* (blog), *The Holy See*, May 25, 1995, http://w2.vatican.va/content/john-paul-ii/it/encyclicals/documents/hf_jp-ii_enc_25051995_ut-unum-sint.html.

Rahner, Karl, Cornelius Ernst, and Kevin Smyth. *Sacramentum Mundi: An Encyclopedia of Theology, Vol. 2*. New York: Herder and Herder, 1968.

Rausch, Thomas P. "Catholics and Pentecostals: Troubled History, New Initiatives." *Theological Studies* 71 (December 2010) 926–50.

Robeck Jr., Cecil M. and Amos Yong. *The Cambridge Companion to Pentecostalism*. Cambridge, NY: Cambridge University Press, 2014.

Root, Michael. "The Unity of the Church and the Reality of the Denominations." *Modern Theology* 9 (October 1993) 385–401.

Schenk, Richard. "The Unsundered Net: Benedict XVI and the Prospects of Ecumenism." *Dialog: A Journal of Theology* 44 (September 2005) 292–96.

Bibliography

Spadaro, Antonio. "The Prosperity Gospel: Dangerous and Different." *Free Articles* (blog), *La Civiltà Cattolica*, July 20, 2018, https://laciviltacattolica.com/the-prosperity-gospel-dangerous-and-different/.

Ukpong, Donatus Pius. *Nigerian Pentecostalism: Case, Diagnosis and Prescription*. Uyo, Nigeria: Fruities Publications, 2008.

Zachman, Randall C. *John Calvin and Roman Catholicism: Critique and Engagement, Then and Now*. Grand Rapids: Baker Academic, 2008.

Index

Abe, G. O., 17
Acts of the Apostles, 37, 101
Africa
    ecumenism in, 103–7
    Pentecostalism in, 40–48, 93–95
African Americans, Pentecostalism and, 43–44
African Independent Churches (AICs), 29–30, 42–44, 92–95, 102
age groups
    data on Pentecostalism and, 3
    response to Christian tradition by, 7–8, 115, 117
    response to ecumenism by, 9–10, 120
    survey participants by, 3–4, 109
Akinwale, Anthony, 85–87
Aladura Churches, 29, 40, 46
American revivalism, 38
Anabaptists, 27, 37–38, 101
Anderson, Allan, 31–32, 37–38
Anglicanorum Coetibus, 77
Anglicans, 26–27
anti-intellectualism, in South African Pentecostalism, 98
apostles, ecumenism and early church of, 17–19
apostolic church, Pentecostalism and, 31–32, 36–38, 101–3
Asia, Pentecostalism in, 40
Assembly of God Church, 42
Athenagoras (Patriarch), 24–25
Augustine, Bishop of Hippo, 63
authority, in Pentecostal movement, 14
Ayegboyin, Deji, 18

Azusa Street mission, 43

Babel, Pentecost as reversal of, 16
baptism, in Pentecostalism, 90, 101
Barret, David, 40n.11
Bea, Cardinal Augustin, 67–69
Benedict XVI (Pope), 75–77
Bergoglio, Jorge Mario. *See* Francis (Pope)
Boko Haram, 59
Bonny, Johan, xixn.2
Bräuer, Martin, 77
Brie, Mircea, 21
Byamungu, Gosbert T. M., 52–53, 104–7, xx

Calvin, John, 25–27, 26–27
Catholic Church
    African Independent Churches and, 29–30
    Charismatic Renewal in, 39, 43
    Counter-Reformation and, 20
    ecumenism and, 18–21, 23–25, 29–30, 33–34, 64–81
    history of ecumenism in, 67–69
    Pentecostalism and, 38–39, 92–93
    post-Vatican II ecumenism in, 69–81
    Reformation and, 25–28
    separation of East and West in, 18–19, 23–25, 70
    teaching authority of, 102

Index

Catholic-Protestant Western Christianity, 25
charismata
    challenges of, 61–62
    Pentecostalism and, 37–39
charismatic movement, 43
Charismatic Renewal, 39
Christian Association of Nigeria (CAN), 29–30
Christian Council of Nigeria, 29
Christianity
    active social role of, 8
    demographic shifts in, 5–10, xxiii–xxiv
    in developing world, xix–xxi
    ecumenism and fragmentation of, 19–23
    ecumenism and growth of, 23–25
    impact of Pentecostalism on, 1–3, xvii–xviii
    models of unity for, 84n.2
    pastor's call to, 11–16
    Pentecostalism and, 38–40
    Reformation and, 25–28
    response to traditions, grouped by country and sex, 7–8
    traditional ties by country and sex, 5–6
Church
    definitions of, 85–95
    objectives of, 12–13
Church of England, 26–27
Church of God in Christ, 42
class structure, survey participants and, 3–4
Clement of Rome, 37
Clement VII (Pope), 27
clergy, training for, 98–99
clerical order, 102n.11
    in Pentecostal movement, 14
Conger, Yves, 33, 69
Congregation for the Doctrine of the Faith (CDF), 75
corruption, Pentecostalism and, 49–53
Council of Chalcedon, 24
Council of Constantinople (3), 24
Council of Florence, 24
Council of Lyons, 24
Counter-Reformation, 20
country
    data on Pentecostalism grouped by, 3, 110
    previous religious affiliation and, 4, 111–13
    response to Christian tradition by, 7–8, 114–17
    response to ecumenicalism by, 8–10, 119–20
    traditional Christian ties by, 5–6
creeds, Pentecostal skepticism concerning, 101–2
cross as icon, Pentecostalism and removal of, 88–95
crusade of 1202–1204, 24

data analysis, overview of, 1–16
De Lubac, Henri, 69
Decree on Eastern Catholic Churches, 66
democratization, Pentecostalism and, 53–61
developing nations, ecumenical Christianity and, xvii–xxiv
diabolicialism, African Pentecostalism and, 55–61
Diet of Worms, 26
doctrinal divide, Pentecostalism and, 100–101
Duffy, Eamon, 74

early Christianity, Pentecostalism and, 36–37
Eastern Orthodox Christianity, 25
Ecumenical Association of Third World Theologians (EATWOT), xxi
ecumenical councils, 24
ecumenism
    Benedict XVI (Pope) and, 75–77
    Catholics and, 18–19, 23–25, 29–30, 64–81
    current trends in, 25, xvii–xx
    decline of, 33–34
    etymology, 20–21

Index

Francis (Pope) and, 77–80
future Pentecostalism and, 58–61
John Paul II and, 71–75
origins of, 17–19
pastors' understanding of, 12
Paul VI and, 70–72
Pentecostal barriers to, 29–34, 87–95, 104–7
postcolonialism and, 94–95
post-Vatican II trends in, 69–81
in pre-Vatican II era, 67–69
response by country and sex to, 8–10
in West Africa, 21–23, 30–34, 83–95, 122–27
Einfuhrun in das Chrestentum, 75
Ephesians, 4:15–16, 35
Ethiopian movement, 44
Eucharistic Prayer, 96
Evangelical Fellowship, 29
evangelicalism
  disconnect with social involvement and, 32
  Pentecostalism, 14, 92–95
Evangelium Gaudium (EG) (Pope Francis), 77

Faggioli, Massimo, 74, 76–77, 80
"faith gospel," 51
fieldwork on Pentecostalism, overview of, 1–16
Figueroa, Marcelo, 88–89
first council of Jerusalem, 17
Francis (Pope), 77–80
Fuss, Michael, 39, 95

Gaudium et Spes, 74
Gbagbo, Laurent, 49–50
gender
  data on Pentecostalism and, 3
  previous religious affiliation and, 4, 111–13
  response to Christian tradition by, 7–8, 114, 116
  response to ecumenicalism by, 8–9, 119

survey participants' distribution by, 5–9, 109
traditional Christian ties by, 5–6
General Overseers (GOs), disconnect with social involvement by, 32
German Pietism, 38
Ghana
  factionalism of Pentecostalism in, xviii–xix
  Islamic extremism in, 59
  research issues in, 3
  survey participants from, 3–4
Gifford, Paul, 49, 51
Global South, Pentecostalism in, 40–43
Gospel of John, Jesus' prayer in (John 17:20–23), 11–12
Gospel of Matthew, 28:18–19, 11
gospel of prosperity, 87–95
governance
  in Pentecostal movement, 14
  Pentecostalism and, 49–53
"great commission," pastor's calling as, 11, 14
Gros, Jeffrey, 65

Haight, Roger, xviii
Henry VIII (King of England), 26–27
Holiness Movement, 38
Hollenweger, Walter, 40–42, 104
Houphouet-Boigny, Felix, 50n.39
humanism, 25

Ibrahim, Ibrahim Yahaya, 58–59
Idowu, Bolaji, 59–60
Ignatius of Antioch, 37
indigenous culture, Pentecostalism and influence of, 44–46
The Institute of the Christian Religion, 27
International Church of the Four Square Gospel, 42
Irenaeus, 37
Islamic extremism, 25
  Pentecostalism and, 58–61
Ivory Coast, Pentecostalism in, 49–50

Index

Jesus' prayer (John 17:20–23), 11–12
John Paul II (Pope), 71–75
John XXIII (Pope), 21, 24, 64–65, 68–69
Johnson, Todd, 40n.11
Judaism
    Benedict XVI and, 75–76
    ecumenism and, 17–19
    John Paul II's rapprochement with, 74–75
Justin Martyr, 37

Kalu, Ogbu, 44–46, 56–57
Kasper, Cardinal Walter, 39
Kerekou, Mathieu, 49

Leeming, Bernard, 28n.28, 100
liberation, Christianity and, xxii–xxiv
Lowery, Mark D., 18, 20
Lumen Gentium (Dogmatic Constitution on the Church), 71
Luther, Martin, 25–28, 38

Macchia, Frank, 30–31, 99–100
McBrien, Richard, 24
McDonnell, Killian, xx, xxii
media events, gospel of prosperity and, 88–95
metanoia, xxii
Methodism, 38
Meyer, Birgit, 46–47
migrant diaspora, Pentecostalism and, 47–48
ministry of Pentecostal movement, 14
mission of Pentecostal movement, 14
missionaries, Pentecostalism and influence of, 46, 104–7
monothelitism, 24
Montanism, 37
Montini, Giovanni Cardinal. *See* Paul VI (Pope)
Munster, Thomas, 38
Mussolini, Benito, 92

mysticism, African Pentecostalism and, 55–61

Nazirite Church, 46
Ndiokwere, Nathaniel I., 93n.26
Nel, Marius, 98
neo-Pentecostalism, 43
    ecumenism and, 30–33
    future in West Africa of, 53–61
    pneumatology rhetoric of, 85–87
    political and social impact of, 49–53
    in West Africa, 97–103
new religious movements, suspicion of unity in, 90–91, 93–95
New Testament
    Anabaptists and, 101
    ecumenism and, 18–19
    Pentecostalism and, 37
N'Guessan, Konstanze, 50
Nigeria
    Christianity in, 29
    factionalism of Pentecostalism in, xviii–xix
    Islamic extremism in, 59
    Pentecostalism in, 29–30
    research issues in, 3
    social and political impact of Pentecostalism in, 50–51
    survey participants from, 3–4
Nigerian Anglican/Roman Catholic Commission (NARCC), 29
Nostra aetate, 69
Nwosuh, Emeka, 87–88, 90

Oduyoye, Mercy Amber, xxiii
Old Testament, ecumenism and, 17–19
Omenyo, Cephas, 36, 48, 54–55
Onaihekan, John Cardinal, 62
Onyewuenyi, Innocent, 107
oral interviews, analysis of, 10–11
orality, 41–43
Origen, 37
Orthodoxy doctrine, 28n.28
Oxford History of Christianity, 27

Index

papal primacy and infallibility, Pentecostal skepticism concerning, 102
Parham, Charles, 43n.21
pastors
    on appeal of Pentecostalism, 13
    calling as "great commission" for, 11–12
    on church objectives, 12–13
    on factionalism in Pentecostalism, 13
    questionnaire for, 11–16
patriarchates, ecumenism and growth of, 23–25
Paul VI (Pope), 24–25, 70–72
Peel, J. D. Y., 47
Pentecostalism
    in Africa, 40–48
    African Independent Churches and, 29–30, 92–93
    Akinwale's analysis of, 85–87
    appeal of, 13
    Byamungu's discussion of, 104–7
    Catholics and, 38–39, 92–95
    church structure and, 85–95
    classification of, 42–43
    ecumenism and, 29–34, 87–95, 104–7
    expansion of, 36, 39
    factionalism in, 13, xviii–xix
    foundations of, 14, 36–37
    future of, 15, 97–103
    geographical breakdown of, 41–43
    models of, 90–95
    modern trends in, xvii–xviii
    in Nigeria, 29–30
    origins and evolution of, 43–48
    pastoral approach in, xxiv–xxv
    persecution of, 92–95
    political and social impact of, 48–53
    postcolonialism and, 94–95
    rotational leadership in, 30
    sustainability of, 97–103
    in West Africa, 83–95, 122–27
Pentecôtistes nouvelle génération (PNG), 52–53
personality cult, in African Pentecostalism, 55–57

Pillay, Jerry, 33n.37, xix, xxiii–xxiv
pluralism, ecumenism and, 20
pneumatology rhetoric, 85–87
polarization, in Pentecostalism, 90–95
political engagement, Pentecostalism and, 32, 48–53
Pontifical Council for Culture, 71
Pontifical Council for Dialogue with Non-Believers, 71
Pontifical Council for Interrreligious Dialogue for Non-Christians, 70–71
pontifical secretariat for Christian unity, 65
postcolonialism, African religious denominations and, 94–95
poverty
    Christianity and focus on, xx–xxii
    in developing nations, xxiii–xxiv
    Pentecostalism's impact on, 1–3, 59–61, 97–103
previous religious affiliation
    by country, sex and age group, 5, 111–13
    survey participation and, 3–4, 111–13
Prior, John Mansford, 51–52
prophets, ecumenism and, 17–19
Public Religion Research Institute (PRRI), 83

Quattara, Alassane, 50
questionnaires
    data analysis of, 3–10
    design and distribution of, 2–3
    doctoring of, 3
    Pastor's/GO's questionnaires, 11–16
    samples of, 121

Ratzinger, Joseph, 69, 75. *See also* Benedict XVI (Pope)
Rausch, Thomas, 32–33, 40–41, 43n.20–21, 99
reaching out, reaching in, and releasing (the 3 *Rs*), 14
refondation, Pentecostalism and, 50

Index

Reformation
  ecumenism and, 18–20, 23
  history of, 25–28
  Pentecostalism and, 37–38, 40–41
research methodology for Pentecostalism, xxv–xxvii
  overview of, 1–16
Robeck, Cecil M., 42n.17, 84n.2, 90–95
Root, Michael, 22

Schenk, Richard, 75–76
Schillebeeckx, Edward, 69
schisms, ecumenism and, 23–25
Scholasticism, 25, 37
Scripture Unions (SUs), 11, 54
Sierra Leone
  Islamic extremism in, 59
  Pentecostalism, 51
  survey participants from, 3–4
social role of Christianity
  Pentecostalism and, 32, 48–53
  response by country, sex, and age to, 8, 118
South America, Pentecostalism in, 40
Southern African Hemisphere,
  Christianity's shift to, xxiii–xxiv
Spadaro, Antonio, 88–89
spiritism, African Pentecostalism and, 55–56
spirituality
  gospel of prosperity and, 87–95
  in Pentecostalism, 99–100
Sub-Saharan Africa, Pentecostalism in, 38, 58–61

Tertullian, 37
theological training, Pentecostalism and, 98–99
third world, expansion of Pentecostalism in, 41–43

tongue-speech, 30–31, 37
traditional African religions, 59–61

Uhuru, Christianity and, 1–3
Unam Sanctam, 65–66
Unitatis Redintegratio, 69–70, 72
Ut Unum Sint, 72–74

Vanhoozer, Kevin J., 1–16
Vatican Councils I and II
  ecumenism and, 19–21, 24, 33, 64–66, 80–81
  Paul VI and, 70–71
Vondey, Wolfgang, 55–56, 103–4

Wesley, John, 38
West Africa
  ecumenism in, 21–23, 30–34, 83–95, 122–27
  expansion of Pentecostalism in, 30, 40–43, 61–62
  factionalism of Pentacostalism in, xviii–xix
  future of Pentecostalism in, 53–61
  neo-Pentecostalism in, 97–103
  Pentecostalism in, 83–95, 122–27
  political and social impact of Pentecostalism in, 48–53
Wojtyla, Josef Karol. *See* John Paul II (Pope)
World Council of Churches (WCC), 19

Yahwism, ecumenism and, 17–19

Zachman, Randal, 26n.25
Zionist Church, 46
Zwingli, Ulrich, 25–27

www.ingramcontent.com/pod-product-compliance
Lightning Source LLC
Chambersburg PA
CBHW051105160426
43193CB00010B/1324